Christian

Christian

Its Meanings in
an Age of Future Shock

Malcolm Boyd

HAWTHORN BOOKS, INC.
Publishers/NEW YORK

Acknowledgments

The publisher gratefully acknowledges permission to reprint from articles by Malcolm Boyd that originally appeared in the following publications:

The Outlook section of *The Washington Post*, copyright © 1973, 1974 by *The Washington Post* —excerpts on pp. 57-63 from "Talking with America," September 9, 1973; pp. 112-17 from "Nixonspell," May 20, 1973; on pp. 159-66 from "Martin Luther King: Man, Mystery," January 20, 1974.

Newsday—excerpts on pp. 43-47 from "On Criticizing Israel: Part II," Viewpoints page, January 18, 1974; pp. 72-79 and 84-85 from "Graham and the Gospel," Ideas page, August 26, 1973; pp. 103-10 from "Jesus, Betrayed Again," Ideas page, July 15, 1973.

The Arts and Leisure section of *The New York Times* Sunday edition, copyright © 1971/72 by The New York Times Company—excerpts on pp. 99-103 from "A Priest Says, 'It Doesn't Have a Soul,' " October 24, 1971; pp. 121-26 from "To Worship and Glorify God," November 12, 1972.

The Christian Century—excerpts on pp. 51-56 from "Superstate with a Superchrist," October 2, 1974; pp. 64-70 from "Watts Revisited," July 31, 1974; pp. 173-81 from "A Personal Half-Century," June 5, 1974.

Ms., copyright © 1974 Ms. Magazine Corporation—excerpts on pp. 137-43 from "Who's Afraid of Women Priests?", December 1974.

Excerpts on pages 12-13, 81, and 131-32 from *A Theology of Liberation* by Gustavo Gutierrez. Copyright © 1973 by Orbis Books. Reprinted by permission of Orbis Books.

Excerpts on pages 87-88, 88-89, and 95 from *Are You Running with Me, Jesus?* by Malcolm Boyd. Copyright © 1965 by Malcolm Boyd. Reprinted by permission of Holt, Rinehart and Winston, Publishers. Permission to reprint also granted by William Heinemann LTD, publishers of *Are You Running with Me, Jesus?* in the British Commonwealth and Empire market excluding Canada.

Excerpt on pages 147-48 from *Malcolm Boyd's Book of Days* by Malcolm Boyd. Copyright © 1968 by Malcolm Boyd. Reprinted by permission of Random House, Inc.

CHRISTIAN

Library of Congress Catalog Card Number: 74-31633
ISBN: 0-8015-1270-0

First printing, June 1975
Second printing, July 1975

To
MISHKENOT SHA'ANANIM
Jerusalem

Contents

Introduction

A fire crackled in the grate behind him, warming the cold office as he faced me across a massive desk that was piled high with papers.

He was a tall man with a kingly mien. White hair covered his head. He treated me kindly and without the least sign of urgency on this, the last day he would spend in his office. As we chatted, I saw him caught halfway between two worlds, one of high prestige and heavily punctuated involvement, the other of renunciation and introspection.

His books were packed in boxes neatly stacked in a hallway outside his office. Our interview took place early on a Saturday; the next morning he would preach his final sermon in the cathedral next door, and on Monday morning the seventy-two-year-old archbishop would catch a plane taking him to a town many thousands of miles away, where he planned to live for the rest of his life.

It seemed that he trusted me. But then again surely he didn't have to give much of a damn concerning what he told me. By the time it was published, he would be gone. Probably I was the last person who would ask him questions, jotting down notes on a pad of paper.

"Religion is being burned and purified," his voice thundered at me, containing at least the hot embers of an old fire. "Whether religion is being cremated or cleansed by fire, I don't know."

We sat together in the limbo of an unhurried silence for a few moments.

"The Jews are going to recall us to Jesus," he said. "They are now studying him in his Jewishness. Taking him as a man without our theological definitions. But this is the way the first Christians were. I think we're going to drop a lot of the ontological definitions we picked up from the Greeks."

The archbishop's bushy eyebrows worked. He looked at me through slightly watery blue eyes, and his fingers played with a rubber band.

"Jesus to me does mean the ever-living one rather than the preexistent one. I don't worry too much about what went on before his birth. It is his continuing influence in my life and the life of the world that really counts. The Resurrection is a seminal event."

When I silently wondered if he were going to talk about these matters in his sermon the next morning, the archbishop responded to my thoughts.

"I can't say things like these to the faithful people inside the church," he remarked. "It would offend them. They wouldn't be able to understand. It's a great pity. I have always told them what they were able to comprehend. Yet have I therefore remained a stranger to them? Oh, if we could be open and completely honest with one another inside the church.

"One thing has become clear to me. We Christians have tended to put Jesus in the place of God. To me, the key to him lies in St. Paul's phrase, 'God was in Christ.' We're right in focusing our attention on Jesus as long as we allow him to take us to God. A guideline. But if we stop before that, we're betraying him. For God was the great centrality to him."

I thought I should probably stand up now and shake his hand, leaving him to the last-minute touches on the sermon that he would preach.

"I can't say God without Christ or Christ without God," the archbishop went on. "But God in Christ. I can't find anything more expressive than Christ's definition of God. It's no lack of loyalty to him to go on to the God from whom he came and to whom he went.

"Here our involvement with other religions comes in. If God is the great Father, he must be working wherever there is good."

The archbishop's ring lay heavily on one of his fingers.

"The churches must somehow get down to a new bit of tough thinking. We are failing to translate the second great Commandment, "Thou shalt love thy neighbor as thyself," from the individual into the corporate. Classes and nations have got to be good neighbors—investors, consumers, political parties, governments. Our refusal to do this is holding us up."

His forty-five long years of ministry—nearly as long as my entire life—were a vivid image in my mind. His face was a seeming mixture of peace and disturbance. I yearned to know the whole of his experience and his feeling. Could he place his hand upon my head, I wondered, and somehow transmit to my consciousness the apostolic succession of what was contained in his heart, his love, his evident discipleship of one called Jesus Christ?

The archbishop left me with no easy grace but a challenge, a dilemma, a burden that he shared.

"Perhaps people have to forget all we've ever told them about God so they can come to him anew," he said. "False religion must be destroyed."

Not easy words. I suppose I had selfishly wanted easy words from a patriarchal Christian leader who was stepping down, relinquishing his yoke.

In a few moments I had said good-bye to him. The

Malcolm Boyd is seen atop the Mount of Olives in Jerusalem.

archbishop courteously walked with me to the door of his office. Someone else sat on a bench outside, waiting to go in. I made my way past the boxes of books awaiting shipment and destined to accompany the archbishop into his retirement.

Bread-and-butter issues were on my mind. Commentators had been talking during the preceding few days about the crisis of leadership in world politics. Bread-and-butter issues were no longer being addressed, they said, in any sort of a gut or realistic way. In other words, highfalutin words, rituals, and methods no longer worked, these commentators said, whether the scene was Europe, America, Asia, or Africa.

Had the archbishop discussed bread-and-butter issues with me? I thought he had—certainly from his vantage point. For he had discussed faith itself. Church establishments often seem to prefer not to do this. Their refusal or inability renders possible the irony; for example, that the 1974 José Quintero production on Broadway of Eugene O'Neill's *A Moon for the Misbegotten* was the best telling of the Passion story one could presently find anywhere, in or out of any church.

In addition, I had just discovered the popular and highly readable Harry Kemelman "Rabbi" mystery stories (*Friday The Rabbi Slept Late, Saturday The Rabbi Went Hungry, Sunday The Rabbi Stayed Home*, and so on). Ironically, this faithful portrait of suburban U.S. synagogue life was, quite aside from particular religious references and description of rituals, indistinguishable from the dynamics of Christian parish life in a church down the street. So bread-and-butter issues go by the board. People are far more concerned, Kemelman accurately tells us, with the rabbi's—or minister-priest's—appearance. Is his suit pressed? Does he look neat? How does he stack up against the other clergy in the neighborhood for having, say, a deep, godly voice? Indeed, is the synagogue—or parish—a socially respectable one? Are the windows nice? Is the floor swept clean? Can one's wife get on an important committee and have her name mentioned in the local newspaper columns? Where is the money? Are the big shots here?

However, the bread-and-butter issues concerning the communication and practice of faith remain the central ones because they deal with life and death. The traditional Holy Week service of Tenebrae, when candles are extinguished, one by one, until one candle alone flickers while the rest of the church is enveloped in the darkness of night, always graphically reminds me of this reality.

What were the bread-and-butter issues for the archbishop? They were very few, I felt.

I had to ask myself what were the bread-and-butter issues for me?

Christian

Malcolm Boyd stands before the Western (Wailing) Wall in Jerusalem.

I

Jew and Christian: In Common

I caught a New England limousine for New York's Kennedy Airport. The car was filled, except for an empty seat next to the driver. I occupied it. The driver asked us which flights we were taking that day. The names were called out. United. American. TWA.

"El Al," I said. El Al is the airline of Israel.

We motored along in silence for a while.

"Last week I drove two Jewish girls who just got back from Israel," the driver said. "They had fresh fruit they had brought home with them. They were telling me that the fruit was confiscated. They couldn't bring it through customs."

Nobody in the limousine was talkative, but I allowed as how customs could be difficult. The driver lapsed into silence.

"I was reading a book," the driver said after another half-hour had passed. "It was about Germany. Most of the Germans, according to the book, didn't know what was happening. It was just a few Nazis who were guilty, and they didn't tell the rest of the people."

Neither I nor anyone else felt like making a response to the driver's remark, so the trip continued quietly and un-

1

eventfully. El Al was the car's first stop at the airport. But moments before the limousine reached the entrance to the terminal, the driver turned his head toward me and asked, "Why do you Jews want to go to Israel?"

In 1964 I had visited Israel briefly for the first time. However, I was a member of a tour whose group dynamics sadly took precedence over getting involved with the land and the people I wished to see. When the opportunity arose to visit Israel under far more auspicious circumstances in the spring of 1972—exactly five years after the Six-Day War—I accepted the invitation with alacrity.

The El Al dinner aboard the plane was kosher, as I should have known it must be, but I forgot the meal included meat. When fruit was offered to the passengers after the meal, I asked, "Is there some cheese?"

The stewardess opened her mouth to say no. I knew the answer, and why, and was suddenly embarrassed. A kosher meal cannot combine meat with milk or any food that contains milk. This is according to strict rules of Orthodox Judaism. Why had I been so stupid and insensitive, I asked myself, to commit that gaffe? I must watch myself and not be an intolerable tourist.

My seat companion on the flight was a taciturn young man who never spoke a word to anyone, not even to a stewardess in acknowledgment of being given dinner or in response to questions. He appeared to be an athlete or a soldier, for his body was muscular and he conveyed an impression of physical strength. I assumed he spoke another language and dismissed the matter from my mind.

I had homework aboard the plane. Once inside Israel, I intended to explore the matter of Jewish-Arab relations there. One publication I had with me was a transcript of conversations between Arab and Jewish students at the Hebrew University.

Now the time was 2 A.M. Most of the other passengers, including my seat companion, had apparently gone to sleep as I began to read the document.

"Why are you reading that?" the young man abruptly asked. He spoke English with only the slightest accent. He explained that he was a Sabra, a native-born Israeli, who had been visiting relatives in the United States as their guest during a holiday. I put aside my reading in favor of a long conversation.

It was his arrogance—there is no other word to describe his facade—that initially struck me. As we talked, this outer roughness or seeming harsh unfriendliness gave way to warmth, marked by an abrupt directness in getting to the heart of issues or ideas. We became friends. I liked the qualities I found in him.

I thought of him immediately several days later when I visited Yad Vashem, the Holocaust memorial in Jerusalem. Buchenwald. Auschwitz. Dachau. The names of the death camps where six million Jews perished are written inside Yad Vashem. Ashes of victims' bodies were brought here from the camps. A flame burns by the grave.

I found written upon a wall the words from a letter written by Opher Feniger, a parachutist and member of Kibbutz Givat Haim, who fell in the Six-Day War:

> I cannot say that I feel what they felt, they the doomed who lived without hope in the shadow of death, but I sense it in all the hell and the terror that shows in their Jewish eyes, the wise eyes that know so much suffering behind the electrified fence—I have the feeling that out of all the horror and the hopelessness there rises and grows up in me an enormous force to be strong, strong even to tears, strong and sharp as a knife, silent and threatening—that is how I want to be. Only when

I am strong will that look disappear! If we will all be strong! Strong and proud Jews! No longer will we be led to the slaughter.

The young Sabra on the plane had made "that look disappear" in his face, his manner, and style. He was "strong and sharp as a knife, silent and threatening," yet he carried this with an innate relaxation and overpowering sense of confidence.

There was the aspect of—what can I call it?—a personal odyssey that contributed to my wanting to visit Israel. It was an almost lost fragment in my history. Three of my grandparents were Anglo-Saxon Protestants. The fourth, removed early from my consciousness by a divorce followed by death, was a Jew. I knew that in Nazi Germany this fact of my having a Jewish grandparent could have led to my imprisonment, possibly to my death. What significance could it hold for me now? Was it simply a meaningless statistic that brushed against my life? It seemed to be a unique time to examine the roots that comprised my life; indeed, my identity as a person.

I grew up a Christian and remain one by the commitment of faith and personal belief. During high school and college days I thought of Judaism as an alien faith utterly distant from my own experience. (Sunday school raised the insistent question, hadn't the Jews killed Christ?)

Jewishness as a life-style often seemed forbidding and even odd. What was kosher food? What in the world was a bar mitzvah? What tradition did Jews observe at Christmas? My separation from Jews, already a fact of life, increased in college when I joined a fraternity. It was Christian; there were separate Jewish fraternities, and the twain never met.

I remember a voting session in my fraternity when new pledges came under consideration. A particular name was called.

"He has a car," one member said. Applause.

"The guy's an athlete."

"He's sexy, man." Whistles. Laughter.

"He's got grades."

"You guys, listen. I'm serious about this. He looks Jewish. You know? He's got all that kike hair on his face that doesn't shave clean. I say no."

The prospective fraternity brother was blackballed. I said nothing in protest.

During my days as a college student, I was invited home over a Christmas holiday by a girl whom I dated. To my consternation, I encountered another example of prejudice toward Jews, an overt expression of anti-semitism that was couched behind an easygoing smile. On Christmas Day the entire family was seated around a table laden with foods. A fire crackled in a grate. The atmosphere was *gemütlich*, one of cheer and friendliness. The girl picked up a morsel of leftover food on her plate and started to place it inside the mouth of the family dog that was begging.

"Don't give that damned Jew any more to eat," her mother said, smiling warmly. "He's had too much already."

The specter of anti-Semitism had recently become locked inside my mind. For my world-view now included Hitler and his mobs, goose-stepping Nazi soldiers marching in shiny black boots, Herr Goebbels who acted like a devil and resembled an ascetic monk, and a rich civilization that was bent on persecution and its own ruin.

The staccato quality of Hitler's voice stuck in my awareness. It was accompanied by the rhythmic, measured cries out of thousands of Nazis' throats, growing in intensity until a blood sacrifice insinuated itself into one's own blood. The imagery of flailing whips and broken bones caused me to cower in evocative fear as if before an incensed serpent-god that demanded one's essence, identity, blood, body, mind, soul—one's very being.

Outwardly none of these thoughts or sensations surfaced

in my existence. Upon graduation from college I went to work in Hollywood for nearly ten years. There, to my surprise, I discovered that the people close to me were Jews. Now I proceeded to explore the boundaries of an industry that included movies, radio, and a new invention called television. But deep changes took place in my interior life, my goals underwent a profound transformation, and in 1951 I left Hollywood to enter a theological seminary.

I wanted to open up my life to God's holiness and full human solidarity.

> Oh, my soul
>> Sing, soul
>> Soul, sing
>> Cry, soul, laugh
>
> Oh, my soul
>> Burn, soul
>> Soul, burn
>> Cry, soul, laugh
>
> Oh, my soul
>> Pray, soul
>> Soul, pray
>> Cry, soul, laugh
>
> Oh, my soul
>> Dance, soul
>> Soul, dance
>> Cry, soul, laugh

Psalms and eucharistic devotions undergirded my meditation.

"My soul hath a desire and longing to enter into the courts of the Lord; my heart and my flesh rejoice in the living God. Yea, the sparrow hath found her an house, and the swallow a nest where she may lay her young; even thy altars, O Lord of hosts, my King and my God."

"Teach me thy way, O Lord, and I will walk in thy truth: O knit my heart unto thee, that I may fear thy Name."

"Out of the deep have I called unto thee, O Lord; Lord, hear my voice."

"To the Table of thy most sweet Feast, O loving Lord Jesus Christ, I, a sinner, presuming nothing on my own merits, but trusting in thy mercy and goodness, approach with fear and trembling."

"Soul of Christ, sanctify me. Body of Christ, save me; Blood of Christ, inebriate me; Water from the side of Christ, wash me; Passion of Christ, strengthen me; O good Jesu, hear me; Within thy wounds, hide me."

I had stopped my television and film activities and taken time to go away from the relentless routine of my work. Now I moved gradually into a contemplative life-style and slowly read the Bible from start to finish. Then I took a lot of time to reflect. Finally I decided that I wanted to serve both God and other people by becoming a priest.

"O praise God in his holiness: praise him in the firmament of his power. Praise him in his noble acts: praise him according to his excellent greatness. Praise him in the sound of the trumpet: praise him upon the lute and harp. . . . Let everything that hath breath praise the Lord."

But I remember with some horror a moment inside a church, prior to my departure for the seminary, when my heart constricted and I did not know where to go spiritually, or what to do. Recently I had concluded a long period of agnosticism and struggle with the meaning of faith for an adult human being. I had started to attend a church in Los Angeles occasionally. It scheduled a fund-raising drive. Because I worked in Hollywood, and therefore possessed numerous connections in the entertainment industry, I was asked to obtain celebrities as volunteers to appear at a benefit program in the church. My efforts were aided by those of a close friend, a songwriter who was Jewish.

When I walked into the church on the evening of the benefit, I saw its young rector. Surrounded by a half-dozen high school students, he was gesturing angrily with his hands. His voice boomed out. I heard him say, "I knew that damned Jew would be late."

Apparently the songwriter who had volunteered to help me was a few moments late—as I must have been, too. My idealism was stained and shattered. The joy of the evening benefit—what there had been of it—was drained. I turned and fled. I wondered, what could I do? Religion seemed a terrible thing to me in that moment, something infinitely more complex than I could cope with as an individual who sought communion with God and brotherhood with man.

Years of preparation lay ahead before I would become a priest. Inside the seminary I studied Judaism for the first time. Classes were devoted especially to the Old Testament and church history. I visited, over a period of six months or a year, a different Conservative or Reform synagogue every Friday night, because I wanted to participate in worship with Jews. I had a vision of universal love outside the strictures of my own religious doctrines and practices.

I asked myself: Why does religion separate people instead of unite them? Why must universal love give way, in the priorities of organized religion, to erecting high walls between people in whom God's spirit dwells?

I discovered somewhat painfully that religion is often misused. It becomes self-serving. It loses the dynamic of a holy movement and is transformed into a competitive institution. At this stage, religion tends to look inward to the makings of its own worldly success rather than outward to the needs of others. It even begins to see God in its own image. Its increasingly rigid dogmas limit—in its eyes—the scope of salvation to its own immediate constituency.

The years passed. I graduated from the Church Divinity School of the Pacific in Berkeley, California, went to England to study for a year at Oxford and observe church experiments in Europe, and then did two more years of graduate theological study at the Union Theological Seminary in New York City. Following my ordination as a priest in 1955, I began to serve as rector of St. George's Church in Indianapolis. It was located deep in the inner city.

Across the street from the church was a small, very poor Orthodox synagogue. I was asked to turn on the lights inside the synagogue every Saturday (sabbath) morning, thereby becoming a shabbos *goy*—a Gentile who performs this sort of task for strict religious Jews, who are not allowed to do such things.

When I moved away from the parish to become a college chaplain, I found myself involved in pragmatic interaction and a new dimension of life with an altogether different group of Jews—students and professors. A few of them became intimate friends. One graduate student and I held long discussions during which he explained the dynamics of his personal faith.

"Auschwitz and the simple truth that the Jewish people still exist are the central religious facts in my life," he said. "I can't adjust to myself a truth that encompasses both of them. Hope seems to betray a black truth that is truer than hope. Yet I simply can't live without hope."

He spoke of Yom Kippur: "There is a long blast on the shofar. It represents the slamming shut of the gates of heaven in the pure, straight legend terms in which it is given. Even on Yom Kippur, however, I always permit myself an escape clause. It seems inevitable that I'll get it together on that last moment when my lack of perfect faith will be taken back and forgiven."

The central intention of Yom Kippur is a "new birth," according to Rabbi Marc H. Tanenbaum, director of national interreligious affairs of the American Jewish Committee. Yom Kippur, the Day of Atonement, provides an opportunity to free a person from slavery to sin and enables him or her to start life anew at one with God and one's fellow human beings. Atonement is understood to be a precondition for at-*one*-ment. I remember how the same student spoke of the Passover.

"There is the allegory of the four sons—the smart, the bad, the simple, and the one who didn't know how to ask questions. I always knew, even at the age of eight, that I was in one of the first two."

Soon I entered actively into the tests and turmoil of the civil rights era. I went to jail with Jews. We faced death together on moonlit stretches of lonely southern country roads in the cause of equal rights for blacks, which we defined as obedience to the will of God for human justice.

A rabbi who was with me said that his participation in the movement was directly related to Jewish teaching that any suffering, anywhere in mankind, was therefore his suffering, his concern. This reminded me of Jesus' words in the New Testament. It seemed to me that the rabbi and I shared consciences that had been informed by a common Judeo-Christian heritage. "Let justice roll down like waters," the prophet Amos cried.

Later in the civil rights era of the '60s, I organized a "kneel-in" of black and white Christians to take place on a Good Friday in a dozen segregated, all-white Episcopal churches in Detroit. A friend of mine who was a Jewish student at Wayne State University told me that he wanted to participate. I said no, explaining that the action was religious and, in fact, involved kneeling inside a church. I felt it would be compromising, or wrong, for him to do this.

He argued with me. "It's a *political* action, at least that's how *I* see it, and I want to take part." He did.

However, he made a request of me. It would be necessary

for me to telephone him in order to leave a message concerning the time and place of meeting for various religious
and/or political protestors. "Please leave a message at my
father's office." he told me. "Don't call me at home, OK?
My grandmother doesn't understand our relationship."

Indeed. For wouldn't I proselytize the best Jewish youth?
I have known many of them intimately during the past two
decades. Only once did a youth ask me if he could "begin
instruction" to become a Christian. I told him not to
complicate our friendship with the request, that if he did
desire such instruction surely he could find dozens of people
listed in the telephone directory who would be pleased to
assist him.

I have long thought it was more important to help a Jew
become a better Jew than to turn a good Jew into a good
Christian, a moderate Jew into a moderate Christian, a
good Jew into a moderate Christian, or a moderate Jew into
a good Christian.

What *does* matter is that a Jew or Christian have a sense
of the closeness and the goodness of God—who is actively
loving, and whose loving makes a demand upon people to
love—and that a Jew or a Christian learn how to express
this gift of love actively in responsibility and service to other
people. Salvation is a gift of God, a holy matter that I have
let rest in the providence of God.

Both in civil rights and the peace movement, I have, on
occasion, been jailed, following arrests for "disturbing the
peace," with Jews, various denominational kinds of Christians, and agnostics. We had attempted to act according to
the dictates of conscience that had been informed by a
common Judeo-Christian heritage nurtured by the Bible.

The fact that we were motivated by a yearning to
actively express love in the social sphere, as well as an insistent desire to commit our bodies as an expression of ador-
ation to God and in responsibility for people who were

being maimed in body and spirit, surely meant that we were, by intention, involved together in *an act of worship*. Such a moment has seemed to be purer, despite its acknowledged ambiguities and spiritual shortcomings, than many choreographed moments in the more socially respectable life of organized religion. Today a comprehension of Jewish worship enriches my life and adds a new dimension to it. The celebration of Jewishness as a life force touches me deeply.

One of the bread-and-butter issues of my life is based on this question: What does the Judeo-Christian tradition mean today in the serious practice of morality and religion? In his book *A Theology of Liberation*, Gustavo Gutierrez writes that biblical faith is, above all, faith in a God who reveals himself through historical events, a God who saves in history. Creation, he notes, is regarded in terms of the Exodus, thereby establishing a close link between creation and liberation.

> Yahweh will be remembered throughout the history of Israel by this act which inaugurates its history, a history which is a re-creation. The God who makes the cosmos from chaos is the same God who leads Israel from alienation to liberation. This is what is celebrated in the Jewish passover. André Neher writes: "The first thing that is expressed in the Jewish passover is the certainty of freedom. With the Exodus a new age has struck for humanity: redemption from misery. If the Exodus had not taken place, marked as it was by the twofold sign of the overriding will of God and the free and conscious assent of men, the historical destiny of humanity would have followed another course. This course would have been radically different, as the redemption, the *geulah* of the Exodus from Egypt, would not have been its foundation. . . . All constraint

is accidental; all misery is merely provisional. The breath of freedom which has blown over the world since the Exodus can dispel them this very day." . . . The liberation from Egypt, linked to and even coinciding with creation, adds an element of capital importance: the need and the place for man's active participation in the building of society.*

In 1972 my odyssey took me to Israel for a second visit.

Israel is an issue of importance second to none for many Jews everywhere. A refusal by Christians to accept this, or their inability to comprehend why this is so, constitutes a stumbling block in relations between Jews and Christians.

During the preceding two years, a spokesman for the Ministry of Absorption explained to me, there were more North American immigrants to Israel than in the preceding nineteen years.

The ministry seeks to assist immigrants who come to Israel. They will need work, and Israel can make use of highly skilled manpower for industry. Electronics is thriving. But there is a problem in terms of special skills; for example, it is difficult to absorb lawyers. A lawyer must undergo new training and learning and pass special examinations.

Immigrants need housing, and arrangements for this can be made while they are still abroad. Immigrants must learn how to speak, read, and write Hebrew. Only 15 percent of newcomers from the United States meet this qualification. Training can be pursued in an absorption center or, if an immigrant is young, at a kibbutz.

There are particular problems for Russian immigrants. Russian technology is backward compared to that of the

*From *A Theology of Liberation* by Gustavo Gutierrez. Maryknoll, N.Y.: Orbis Books, 1973, pp. 157-8.

United States and Israel, so new training is necessary. Also there is a dilemma concerning expectation; many Russian Jews have sought immigration for years, and now must make the change from an "exciting" struggle to the exigencies of ordinary, everyday life inside Israel.

In addition, Soviet censorship and limits on information cause Jews who migrate from there to lack prior knowledge about life in Israel.

For newcomers from America, there is often dissatisfaction with the bureaucracy of Israel. These new Israelis point out that there are newer ways of doing things better.

"Israel likes immigration but hates immigrants," Leonard Edelstein of the Jewish Agency jokingly remarked.

Joshua Palmon, who was adviser on Arab affairs to the mayor of Jerusalem, told me, "New immigrants complain to the Jewish Agency about their conditions. Next they complain to the government about their conditions. Next they complain to the government about their high taxes. Then they complain about the new immigrants who receive too much help. Who is not an immigrant? Everybody is an immigrant. It only depends on when."

If I were a Jew, would I want to live in Israel now? The answer would have to depend on numerous factors. I know that. Yet I think that I might. This despite an inevitable and painful decrease in my standard of living, the necessity to learn (and become fluent in) a new language, overwhelming difficulties in finding employment that would be personally fulfilling as well as socially productive, and gambling—there is no other word—that uprooting could be changed into finding far deeper human and spiritual roots.

What did I think of Israel? I found in its life a resurrection following the death of the Holocaust. I liked its energy, pride, earthiness, and vision. I was sometimes baffled by its gigantic materialistic growth in the face of unmet spiritual needs, alarmed by manifestations of its

14

excessive strains and tension, and worried about its frequent insensitivity toward the feelings of the Arabs dwelling inside Israel who defined themselves as Palestinians.

Surely each new generation needs its Amoses and Hoseas, prophets to cleanse social intentions as well as temples, to criticize feasts that distract people from letting justice flow like mighty waters. So I hoped for signs of renewed faith to emerge ever stronger inside Israel.

Inside Jerusalem's Israel Museum I saw Jewish religious objects, instruments of worship used in rituals that were designed to be outward and visible signs or forms of an inward and spiritual grace. These Jewish objects stirred a recollection in my mind of the bar mitzvah scene in the movie *Sunday Bloody Sunday* that had touched a nerve in me.

Movies can move in on people's faces and hands in dramatic close-ups that human eyes can seldom achieve. I was made intensely aware by the film of the older man's remembrance of his own bar mitzvah when he attended his nephew's ceremony. There seemed to be involved a cultural tradition, rooted and imbedded in human bones or even the lines of Jewish faces, that was sorely missing from the Episcopalian confirmation service, whose flaw might be the very loss of finely honed ethnicity in a vast Anglo-Saxon complex of sameness. Or was there also lacking a sharply remembered, and absolutely shared, legacy of corporate suffering as a people?

I soon discovered that Israel is alternately young and old, ancient and modern, thriving and tranquil. For a tourist, a visit here could be an event shrouded in visions of antiquity and his own feelings. He might never come to see Israel itself. For an Israeli, I realized that the nation would have more immediate meanings: getting a place to live amid an inflationary housing market and the rapid flow of immigrants; the likelihood of annual military service in the reserve; and how to protect spiritual integrity and the very vision of Israel in the face of unprecedented material prosperity and the vicissitudes of the haunting Arab-Jewish question.

The pride of the country leaps out at a visitor. At Kibbutz Snir, a new community in Upper Galilee, I chatted with a young Israeli—bearded, wearing an open shirt, short pants and sandals—who had come from South Africa four years earlier.

"I have no connection with the past," he said. "Some people in the world take more than they need. I think that is one of the problems of the world. Not enough people are giving. I am working to be happy. To love. A person has to find out how to love; he must discover himself."

I compared the new kibbutz with older ones. Dov Eshkol, who belonged to the large and prosperous Kibbutz Ayelet Hashahar, recalled earlier and harder days: "We were surrounded by Arabs and living in tents. The area was full of malaria. We wanted a higher standard of living as workers. We wanted to participate in building the country. I was mobilized for seventeen years in the military. On the weekends, I came back and worked here."

One symbol of the 27-year-old nation of Israel is Masada. It is a gaunt mountain overlooking the Dead Sea. Here in ancient times King Herod used slave labor to build a palace that would be unassailable. Later, Jews in revolt occupied the mountain. Under seige for three years by 30,000 Roman soldiers and 70,000 slaves, the 960 Jewish defenders finally committed suicide on the mountaintop in 73 A.D. when confronted by capture. The symbolism of Masada is apparent to modern Israel—a nation with a Jewish population of less than 3 million surrounded by 100 million Arabs.

I walked about, exploring ancient ruins. Then I looked down at the Dead Sea and the sites of the encircling Roman camps far below. Claps of thunder and flashes of lightning startled me out of my reverie, for this was a stormy day.

Atop Masada, the centuries roll together into an unreal present. I walked down the mountain's winding serpentine trail to a car that awaited me.

Another significant symbol of Israel's life is the deceptively quiet Kibbutz Yad Mordechai. It conveys the meaning of Greek tragedy. Named for Mordechai Anilewitz, who perished in the resistance against Nazis in Warsaw in 1943, it was settled by his Jewish compatriots from Poland. Later, in the Israel War of Independence in 1948, Yad Mordechai was surrounded by Egyptian troops, who vastly outnumbered the Israelis. A stubborn defense delayed the enemy for several days, thereby changing the course of the war. Yet finally Yad Mordechai was taken and destroyed. Now rebuilt, it stands as a living monument to the indomitable Jewish spirit.

One day I walked through Tel Azizyate, site of a crucial battle in Upper Galilee that cost many lives in 1967's Six-Day War. I looked at burnt tanks, abandoned bunkers, and barbed wire. The next day I was in the romantic artists' colony of Safed (Zefat), as Israel's paradox continued to assert itself. One night I dined with Bedouins in the tribe of Arab el Hib as hot coals burned in a konoon in our midst. The next noon, in a Druse village (Isfia—which means Windy Days), I conversed in an incredibly quiet room overlooking great valleys with a man who is the son, grandson, and great-grandson of sheiks.

Driving along the Golan Heights, I felt I was in a region inhabited by ghosts. Suddenly, I seemed to be in a top-of-the-world, *Lost Horizon* place, overlooking a crater lake, nestled beneath snowcapped Mount Hermon. Afterwards, mile after mile brought me past battle-scarred, deserted villages and towering, lonely trees.

In Jerusalem, I stood past midnight before the Western (Wailing) Wall. The lines of a letter—written to a kibbutznik at the conclusion of the Six-Day War and later published in the popular Israeli book *The Seventh Day*—expressed poignant feelings with which I found myself able to identify.

> As I stood weeping by the Wall, there wept with me my father, my grandfather and my great-grandfather . . . I caressed its stones, I felt the warmth of those Jewish hearts which had warmed them with a warmth that will forever endure.

On the eve of my departure for Israel, I had talked one evening at Yale with one of the foremost Jewish novelists in America, whose celebrated writing themes have not included either the Holocaust or the Israeli experience.

"I'm going to Israel on Monday," I told him. "Tell me about it—what to do, whom to see."

"I have never been to Israel," he said.

"Don't you want to go?"

"No. There's a boy-scout aspect to it. I'd keep looking into faces that said over and over again 'What have you done for Israel?' I wouldn't like that."

Our conversation came to my mind two weeks later when I sat in the Tel Aviv suburban home of Moshe Shamir, the Israeli novelist and journalist. His wife had poured Scotch on the rocks for us.

"I think many American Jews are afraid of Israel," Shamir said. "Israel is too strong a dilemma. As a Jew, you cannot be an onlooker. You have to participate fully and say good-bye to America and everything in which you have participated. A serious Jew has to answer the question: Why am I not staying in Israel? There is something of desertion, of being a traitor, in not being here."

The definition of "a Jew" came under discussion during my stay in Israel. I reflected upon words written by Arthur Koestler in his novel *Thieves in the Night*: "For Jews were not an accident of the race, but simply man's condition carried to its extreme—a branch of the species touched on the raw."

I chatted in Jerusalem with Rabbi Jack Cohen, director of the B'nai B'rith Hillel Foundation in Israel, who spoke of "the myth of Jewish peoplehood" inside Israel.

"There is the self-identity problem," he said. "Jews are battling among themselves as to who they are. Traditionalist and democratic pluralistic views are worlds apart. Then, too, Jews do not come to Israel just as Jews, but as men and women characteristic of various cultures. It isn't easy to get a Russian Jew to understand what an American Jew is talking about—for example, when he discusses feelings of loyalty to America. To create a people out of this cannot happen overnight."

Reuven Surkis, director of the Israel Historical Society, had come from America to live in Israel. We sipped Cokes in the living room of his modest Jerusalem apartment following dinner with his family.

"We have a problem because we don't know how to run a Jewish state," he said. "We don't know what the Jewishness of running a Jewish state really means. There are some Jews who claim that it must be a theocracy, according to the laws of the Talmud. Others say it is a secular state and a Jewish nation.

"We don't have businesses open on the sabbath, or public transportation. We require our students to study the Bible and Talmud in schools. Is this a coercion or a part of being a Jewish state? We have problems of autopsy. For it is against Jewish law, yet it is a part of running a state."

Moshe Shamir spoke of a "crisis in Judaism" during our conversation in Tel Aviv.

"If Judaism is a religion first and foremost, then it is in a very dead condition," he said. "What saved it from total collapse is Zionism—the opportunity to try again in a different dimension as a nation on its own land. As pure religion, small societies spread all over the world, there is a total bankruptcy. Intermarriage. A lack of believers. Religion becomes a monopoly of small exotic sections. The beautiful thing about Israel is that it started really as a rebellion against Orthodox Judaism. Zionism is a branch of assimilation—let's not use such a strong word. Of secularism. Let's stop praying for the messiah to come and save us. Let's do it with our own hands.

"In a miserably small way, Zionism is a success. The most fascinating aspect of it is the revival of the Hebrew language and the experience of Jewish history. Out of legend or myth has come a unified power, and, with it, something like a religious renaissance. This is not taking place so much in Israel as in Jewish communities outside of Israel. There is a great change of heart in Western Jewry. Personal edification instead of personal philanthropy."

Following the Yom Kippur war in 1973, a number of U.S. journalists wrote that countless American Jews had suddenly been changed into "instant Zionists" because of the intensity of the new threat against Israel. It is the inability on the part of most U.S. Christians to understand the basis of deep Jewish feeling for Israel that stands in the way of open Jewish-Christian dialogue. For more and more American Jews see Jews as *a people.* "A threat to the State of Israel is a threat to the Jewish people, and therefore, the State of Israel is inseparable from the Jewish people," Rabbi Richard G. Hirsch, executive director of the World Union for Progressive Judaism, has noted. "So the State of Israel has restored, and is continuing to restore, the dimension of Jewish peoplehood to all Jews." Signs of this are cited as increased study of the Hebrew language, renewed interest in Jewish culture, and reawakened consciousness of Jewish identity.

Rabbi Jack Cohen said that the people of Israel stand on the threshold of what he called "the second biblical revival."

"If you examine the Bible, to me it is a book that sets forth the problems with which a people has to deal when it comes to settle on its own soil. First, it has to deal with polity concerning other people. Second, it has to develop the ethical values that are necessary to govern the group. Third, it will develop an ideology of man, the universe, God, and so on, which will enable each member of the group to find its place. A certain type of ritual is bound to develop. A secular culture will provide the framework.

"In the State of Israel today, and what preceded it, this process has been going on. The present stage raises a degree of difference between the various people of Israel. The Twelve Tribes were presumably of the same family, while now there are vastly different people with varied problems. It's much easier to be self-critical about the past. The real question is what are you doing now that may make future generations feel self-critical."

The question of self-criticism arose in my conversation in Tel Aviv with the late David Ben-Gurion when I asked him if he had read Amos Elon's book *The Israelis: Founders and Sons.*

"I wish you would not speak of that book," he said. "I wish it had not been written."

What did Elon say in his book that disturbed some people inside Israel and aroused controversy? For one thing, he alluded to the existence of a "spiritual vacuum created by the receding future of the classic Zionist dream, a vacuum that cannot satisfactorily be filled by feats of arms."

In other words, a number of Israelis—and Jews throughout the world—realized that the dream of settling and establishing Israel has been completed. What then, would be the substance of the people's new visions and dreams? What would be the sources of Israel's spiritual and moral power? Could there be peace?

When I spoke with Elon during a visit to his home in Jerusalem, I asked him to comment on the spiritual, or deeply moral, questions that confronted Israel.

"This is a functioning society. A youthful society," said Elon. "What am I afraid to lose? We must never forget that the idea of creating another state was, at the start of Zionism, subservient to creating a better society. Yet Israel is the closest thing to a Greek city-state that exists today.

"Only in raucous, nearly anarchic freedom can you get this kind of strength. There is an electricity in the Israeli society. It comes from a deep spiritual source. It is understood that freedom is more effective than tyranny. There is an element of not wanting to force anybody to do anything. It also comes from an essential gentleness that remains in this society."

Meron Benvenisti, a member of the city council of Jerusalem who had previously resigned, amid controversy, as administrator of East Jerusalem, expressed self-criticism, as well as considerable optimism, during a conversation.

"We know from history that a national movement, once it has begun, cannot be forgotten. A moral danger in Israel is that the occupation of the West Bank will become permanent. However, I don't think this will happen. People would like Israel to be both democratic and Jewish."

I found among Israeli students and young intellectuals a controlled anger concerning organized religion. Several of them said they would like to see a separation between synagogue and state. They felt, nevertheless, a strong identity as being part of the people "of the Book" residing in "the biblical land."

It was difficult for me to determine their definitions of God, for religion is a controversial and often an acrimonious subject. For example, when I visited a new kibbutz near the

Golan Heights, I was told that the young kibbutzim had firmly decided not to build a synagogue there.

A law student at the Hebrew University told me, as we drove early one morning in a car and listened over the radio to to the reading of Scripture that officially opens each day's broadcasting schedule, "I like the reading. It isn't religious or offensive. They place it in an historical perspective. It teaches me something about our history and reminds me of the past which has become the present."

Père Marcel Dubois, a Roman Catholic priest residing in Jerusalem, told me, "We receive from the Jews the revelation of God spoken in history to every man. The Bible is for everyone. The Bible is Jewish existence in history. This universal parable received a concrete actualization in one people."

Yet the sense of religious experience within this people is diffused. For many, Jewishness is a cultural reality first and foremost. Some acknowledge only a pervasive secular strain. Others say that being Jewish means the existence of religious roots, but they aver that it makes no specific religious demands upon them. When the primacy or at least the practice of religion is a basic force in the lives of Jews, this itself is interpreted in the form of Orthodox, Conservative, Reform, or Reconstructionist experience.

I chatted with Amos Elon, at his home which stood across from the Garden of Gethsemane, about religion inside Israel.

"This is like Lourdes, I suppose," he replied. "You can see two processions constantly going on from the windows in this house. You have weary-eyed Jews marching off to the Western Wall in a fetishistic way. There is no holy *place* in Judaism, there is a Holy *One*. And you have these hordes of Swedish, English, and American ladies who are marched off to Gethsemane next door."

Elon, wearing a sweater and slacks, leaned back in his chair and paused for a moment.

"Israel is in many ways the most irreligious country on earth. In America the edge is diluted. Here you have an attempt by the national religious party to impose a way of life on the general public. You can take a taxi on the sabbath but not a bus, which means the rich man can go to the beach in his car that cost fifty thousand pounds but the poor man stays home in his small, hot house. The laws are an infringement of civil laws and civil rights.

"The issue of Jewishness is closely tied in here with the issue of religion and it is also tied in with politics," he said. "What is worrisome about the religious party, which holds the balance of power with 16 percent of the vote, is that it is trying to approve the most chauvinistic and nationalistic position vis-a-vis the Arabs.

"It is the Kahane mentality that says we should rebuild the third temple. If the right wing and the religious should win a majority of votes, no settlement concerning Arabs could be made. Ideally, I would like to see a repartition of Palestine. There's very little chance this will happen. The fact that it didn't work out before doesn't mean that it could not. I would like to have Arabs at least in one part of Palestine to have self-government."

What, if anything, was happening among Israelis in the sense of developing an inner spirituality?

"There is a religious revival of sorts," Elon replied. "Buber has made a comeback among youngsters. Many people say 'Look, we're living without any faith. Something is wrong.' There is some diffuse longing for spiritual values and moral truth. These people believe in God, but not in any organized God. Even if young people have a religious feeling, there is no outlet for it. Israelis grew up in a militantly atheistic background. When a kind of religious revival happens, it is a phenomenon. There are a few young rebels among the rabbinate. Students are interested in them."

I saw signs of what might be interpreted as religious revival in the moral and spiritual introspection that was experienced by many Israelis following the Yom Kippur war. There was an agonizing concern for justice. Also, there was a longing for personal meaning in addition to social definition. For many people, organized religion seemed to stand too far apart from them to offer either real comfort or serious challenge. I wondered from what possibly unexpected source might come religious revival, a shattering force to strike at the very depth of common life and personal being.

I thought of what Rabbi Herbert Weiner wrote in his book *9½ Mystics* about the strengths to be found in Judaism:

> The desire to tie heaven to earth is not, to be sure, an exclusively Jewish goal, but the stubbornness, energy, and measure of success which accompanied this attempted unification in Judaism is perhaps singular in the history of religion. Its secrets, in an age which has seen the bankruptcy of so many attempts to balance spirit and flesh, its exits and reentries, would seem worthy of serious consideration.

For some Israelis, God's grace, providence, or will is inseparable from the State of Israel. How could I relate to this? I have long believed that God is present in life. I felt the presence of God manifested more in the teeming throngs of Jerusalem streets than in the awesome, mysterious, and majestic mountains looming above the Dead Sea. Atop Masada itself, or on the Golan Heights, I felt God less than in the fast-moving human turmoil of downtown Tel Aviv. I felt God's force in Israel, although I do not equate God with Israel *or* America, Jerusalem *or* Washington.

I have trouble identifying God exclusively with any particular religion, faith, denomination, edifice, ritual, creed, prayer, or ecclesiastical hierarchy. God is quite free, I believe. I welcomed in Israel a healthy agnosticism; curiously, it may be the best sign of an actual faith.

Most Israelis whom I met embraced a cause for human survival itself. It was a cause rooted in biblical history, Christian persecution, the Holocaust, and "the resurrection" of the State of Israel. The cause was clearly marked by a never-ending questioning about religion and everything else, an obdurate refusal to bow down before symbols of religious or secular power, and a vestigial awareness of the Holy One—however undefined.

I was certainly more conscious than I had been elsewhere of Jesus' Jewishness, the rituals he knew, and the background out of which he emerged. The mystery of this was, at times, overwhelming. Standing on the Mount of the Beatitudes, I was aware that Jesus had stood there. In Capernaum. On the Via Dolorosa. Atop the Mount of Olives. Before the Western Wall.

Any sober examination of the present meaning of the Judeo-Christian tradition must involve not only taking a close look at the State of Israel, which is the center of world Jewry also for the Jews of the Diaspora, but also at the relations between Jews and Arabs. Christians as well as Jews in America and elsewhere must inevitably reach a position about the questions underlying these relations and know the facts instead of relying on mere emotion.

While visiting Israel in 1972, I knew that, though Arabs and Jews angrily confronted one another in Syria and the Sinai, other Arabs and Jews coexisted inside Israel itself. I wondered what were the realities of this situation and the feelings of the people involved.

I found some surprising answers—individuals on both sides who were striving to interact with one another in new ways.

"I learned the Hebrew language three years ago," a

young Arab electrical engineer in Jerusalem told me. "Now I am able to talk to my Jewish contractor and workers. The name 'Arabic' can lead to hate. So can 'Jewish.' But we must live together."

"Politically speaking, we were conquerors, they the conquered," said a Jewish professor at the Hebrew University who is fluent in Arabic and has close Palestinian friends. "But, socially speaking, both sides have made strides in learning to regard each other as equals."

How deep did this cut? Did it relate significantly to the silent fears and unspoken hurts of the majority of people?

A prominent author in Tel Aviv expressed the latent fear of many Jews when he told me: "If you scratch a Jew in Israel, you'll find a question mark: Will the Arabs allow us, at any point, to stay and remain alive? I think all Arabs are united in the submerged language of the 'buddy' Big Arab nation—the one hundred million of them surrounding us."

Later, inside her East Jerusalem apartment, I chatted with an Arab woman who is a social worker. "I have a Jordanian passport," she said. "I am just a question mark. Nothing. Imagine this feeling: You are in your own country, and at any moment a military order can kick you out, put you in a car, and drive you across a bridge. Jews don't know what they want to do with Arabs like myself on the West Bank. They want the land but not the people."

As I listened carefully to both Jews and Arabs express their opinions concerning the rights of both of these peoples living together inside Israel, the enormity and utter complexity of the problem became ever more of a reality to me. Only a fool would offer facile or simplistic conclusions. The hard fact is that there is logic in both Jewish and Palestinian claims. Intellectual comprehension of such logic, however, does not solve the dilemma of having to adopt a psychological point of view, an emotional reaction, and even a moral posture.

"Arabs and Jews are doomed to live together until the

end of time," a Jewish teacher told me. "We can make it a better prospect instead of an impossible one. Coexistence means keeping a certain distance between Arabs and Jews. I speak of a distance of honor, not a hatred distance.

"This can allow two peoples to live together without being exposed to old abrasiveness. It is tragic that, in effect, Arabs and Jews are in the Alamo today. We don't want to absorb each other. An adequate distance will allow people to smile. It won't go deep in the heart, but it can keep people from killing each other."

The situation inside Israel is by no means static. Change is clearly in the air. For example, a sophisticated young Jew confided to me, "I feel a closer affinity with some East Jerusalem Arabs than with brother Jews coming out of a North African cave culture. On a human basis—that is to say, picking friends—I can choose." Such words doubtless would not have been heard in Israel in 1967 at the time of the Six-Day War.

On the campus of the University of Haifa, I met a young woman who was the first Arab student to be elected to a post in the student government there.

"Students must not learn in separated schools," she said. "I studied with Jews in secondary schools. It is not difficult to be with them. If Arabs and Jews can work together, the eyes of the world will be on us here."

Recently the University of Haifa established a center for Arab-Jewish studies. Near the campus is Bet Hagefen, an Arab-Jewish cultural center. One morning, I joined the members of its women's club during their meeting. They learn Jewish and Arabic cooking, study psychology and flowers, and discuss their husbands and children. Recently 148 people, members of Arab and Jewish families, had filled three buses on a Saturday for an outing on the Golan Heights.

"One of our Jewish women lost her only son," an Arab woman at Bet Hagefen told me. "When she had a remembrance for him at the cemetery, I went. This let her know that some Arabs care about her."

Despite these reports of new interaction between some people as signs of hope, one heard disquieting rumors concerning discrimination against Arabs and their treatment as second-class citizens inside Israel. What about civil rights for Arabs? How much freedom did they have in Israel?

I discovered that there was freedom for an Arab editor to print what he wished in a newspaper, yet there was a sense of trepidation as to what limitations might indeed exist if one should inadvertently push liberty too far. So an Arab can feel he is wrestling with shadows; needless to say, this becomes in itself a curious negation of freedom.

"When I came here, I was very tired," said an Arab graduate student at work on a master's degree at the Hebrew University. "I didn't want to fight. I wanted a quiet corner. Leave me alone, please, is what I was thinking. I didn't want to be suffocated by being placed in an anti-Establishment role. Now I can say what I like, but I don't say much. I know that my roof is lower than a Jew's. It's not a question of university policy. It's a question of people."

Late one night I drank coffee and talked with an Arab newspaper editor inside his office in East Jerusalem.

"Peace must be based on justice for the Palestinian," he said. "The other side must respect my rights if he intends to live with me in peace. I would like to see peace, but I cannot live under occupation forever.

"The opening of the border between the West Bank and Israel after the '67 war is proof that both people can live together in peace. The important thing is to respect the rights, feelings, and culture of each other."

I also talked with Jews who candidly addressed the question of Arab rights.

"How do Arabs feel when they see Jewish symbols on state buildings?" asked an Israeli intellectual. I had joined his family for their sabbath meal. "The real national holi-days par excellence are Jewish ones. The country identifies itself as a Jewish nation. I happen to believe this is good, because I believe that the Jew should have a state. That's why I came here from America to live and take up citizen-ship.

"I'm a humanist also. So I believe there should be auton-omous minority rights. I'm for Arabs to learn as much of Arab history and culture as Jews learn of the Jewish. It's the responsibility of the Israeli government to pour hundreds of thousands of pounds into the development of Arab culture—awareness—identity—raison d'être. An Arab the-ater, an Arab academy of music, an Islamic theological school . . ."

This could be construed as paternalism, despite whatever motivation of decency or goodwill that lay behind it. Many Arabs demand full autonomy, not handouts.

A prominent Jewish lawyer, aware of such deep Arab feelings, told me he does not believe that great changes could yet be made.

"Little things are the only things we can do right now," he said. "But little things can be acts of omission as well as commission. On Independence Day, don't hang flags on the minaret of the Tower of David. We should be sure of ourselves not to impose festivities on what for Arabs is apparently a day of mourning."

A nervous and intense man, he was clearly not a typical Israeli but a highly sensitive and articulate member of a minority that considers self-criticism and even dissent to be an essential part of loyalty to the nation.

"I have to accept the viewpoint of the Arabs to the extent that I realize they are entitled to their own viewpoint," he continued. "If I don't do this, I am a colonialist.

"In 1968, Israelis erected war memorials to dead soldiers. These were in Arab neighborhoods. The Arabs said, 'All right, we want to build our own memorials.' Some of us said OK. There was a terrible outcry among Jews here.

" 'You allow memorials for murderers,' they charged. We said, 'No. They fought for their conviction; we fought on the other side.' This seemed too liberal or pro-Arab to many, but a memorial was erected for the Arab soldiers. The value was a didactic act more than a political one, to make Jews realize what a unified state means."

Actual conditions of life—these including the extraordinary program of building and development within Israel, coupled with the need for labor—dictate the nature of the relationship between Arabs and Jews more than any amount of rhetoric or mere planning.

I heard an apocryphal story concerning what former Prime Minister Golda Meir is supposed to have said: "We construct all of our new buildings with Arab labor and American money for Russian immigrants." This tale smacks of considerable reality. For Arab labor is indeed a necessity in today's Israel, and it serves also vastly to raise the standard of living of Arabs. It forms an acceleration of work contact between Jews and Arabs, thereby bringing together people of quite divergent cultures.

So it undoubtedly tends to increase the liberation of Arab women, bringing them outside their heavy black veils and their subservience to men, and into the world of industry, earning their own wages and maybe even wearing the short skirts so popular with many Israeli women. This cultural collision raises such questions as birth control and the nature of the education that one's children will receive. Neither Jew nor Arab wants any kind of melting pot to occur; however, I see a major question in the offing: What profound effects will cultural intercourse have upon the people involved?

"What is done is far more important than what is wished," said a high Jerusalem official working on Arab affairs. "We are doing our best to give the same services, the facilities of life, to all the people in the city—Arabs and Jews alike. This may sound poetical. But it means keeping the sewage running and preventing smells. Water will run. Garbage will be collected. We are building a new system of roads, water supply, and sewage disposal, along with better school buildings for East Jerusalem."

One saw a different culture, however, driving past an Arab village, as compared with the new stone canyons of sleek Israeli high-rise apartment houses ringing Jerusalem. One heard voices that spoke of Palestinian self-determination—not of sewage disposal.

"The world has solved the Jewish problem while creating an even more difficult one—the Palestinian problem," said an Arab lawyer in Ramallah, a town on the West Bank. I had driven there from Jerusalem to meet him, and we chatted over cups of Turkish coffee.

"What I want is the right of statehood," he said.

His words were echoed by those of an influential Arab journalist who told me, "When the Jews say there is not a place for the Palestinian refugees to come back and live here and at the same time some of their leaders demand that more Jews must come and settle here, it is contradictory. This is a barrier to understanding. The Israelis prefer to make peace with Jordan, not with the Palestinian."

Weighing as carefully as I could what I heard from both Jews and Arabs inside Israel, I reached certain conclusions.

First, it was undeniable that a number of Jews and Arabs were making significant progress in improving interpersonal relations and elevating cooperation over abrasiveness.

Important cultural contributions have occurred toward achieving what is often called "the small peace."

Item: A TV show, "Sami and Susu," became a major factor in changing Jewish images of Arabs. It began as a show in Arabic for Arabs. A couple of years later, complaints were heard from Jewish children and their parents. Why couldn't Hebrew subtitles be used, they asked. Soon they were watching the program, too. New cultural understanding followed.

Item: I attended a rehearsal in Jerusalem's Khan Club of an Arab version of *The Red Shoes.* It had a Jewish director and an all-Arab cast with the exception of one Jewish actor. It was a drama that was later seen by scores of Arab and Jewish children.

Item: It has been suggested that an Arab-Palestinian University be established on the West Bank. This would presumably provide a working center for Arab scholars and intellectuals, who have left Israel in droves, and could inaugurate a new type of Jewish-Arab dialogue under Arab auspices.

Secondly, it was also undeniable that fundamental decisions would have to be made concerning the status of Arabs who reside inside Israel. Many Arabs feel that they are, in fact, excluded from democratic processes. A number of them are content to live side by side with Jews in Israel and do not feel that they constitute a fifth column that seeks to effect needed change by means of violence or revolution. Yet a unified state must provide a felt sense of first-class citizenship for Arabs, an end to occupation, and an inner release that is accompanied by the sure knowledge that an Arab's "roof" is not "lower" than a Jew's.

"I'm still tense when I meet a Jew," the wife of an Arab scholar said. "But I speak frankly. I cannot accept a legalized occupation. I can't come to any real relationship with Israelis. But I'm not against them as human beings."

In the face of this, Amos Elon sounded a warning. "If the occupation should continue, it would bring about a corruption of Israeli society. You cannot maintain a double standard, with first-class citizens and second-class ones. If a blow-up occurs in twenty-five years, it won't be the Arab who will bring the crisis. It will be my son."

Peace inside Israel—in sharp contrast to recurring wars on her borders—is a tantalizing human possibility. But Arabs and Jews would have to work together, with extraordinary mutual candor and sacrifice, in order to achieve it.

In 1974, I returned to Israel in search of an answer to a thorny question: Can there be peace in Jerusalem? The city fits the saying that there is no such thing as peace, but pieces.

A young Israeli woman in panty hose and miniskirt passes an Arab woman whose face is covered by heavy black cloth that also encases her full body. Red poppies dot a hillside sheltering an avant-garde Christian church adjoining seventy thousand Jewish graves that can be traced back as far as twenty-five hundred years.

Not far away a Bedouin shepherd stands just above a fast-moving lane of cars as he watches his goats graze on a clump of grass. Paradoxes fit together here with the precision of an ageless mosaic. Inevitably there is more depth to a scene than a naked eye can behold.

"This is a peaceful place," I remarked as I stood at the foot of the Garden of Gethsemane, gazing at the nearby walls of Jerusalem.

"Not always," replied a Jerusalemite. "This has often been a very fierce battleground—for example, only a few years ago during the Six-Day War."

West Jerusalem's classic vista of stone houses and trees—cypress, pine, pepper, olive, eucalyptus—is punctuated by the speed and rhythm of a modern welfare state. East Jerusalem, Casbah-like in its labyrinth mazes and bazaars, pushes the clock back to days of royal conquest, storied miracles, and eternal mysteries.

Walking along the Via Dolorosa in the Old City of East

Jerusalem—the route followed by Jesus, after he was flogged by the Roman soldiers, toward Golgotha where he was nailed to the cross and died—one is caught up in the myriad vagaries, sounds, and smells of elemental human life. The Stations of the Cross, which depict incidents of Jesus' last walk toward his execution, are marked in walls along the winding, narrow, cobblestone road.

Here one is fittingly thrust into the midst of people who are baking bread, carrying sacks of corn seed, selling produce, animatedly talking in small groups, or dozing in the noon sun. Smells of orange juice, meat cooking on an open stove, moisture of a wet wall, spices from a shop, and even a latrine close to the street assault one's senses. The daylight is blinding, for in Jerusalem the air is clear and there is extraordinary brightness.

"There is peace in Jerusalem," an immigrant to Israel remarked during a recent stroll through the streets of the Old City.

"No," replied a long-time occupant of the city. "We can't have peace in Jerusalem unless the wish for it exists also in Saudi Arabia, the United States, Soviet Russia, the Vatican, Egypt, and Syria."

Jerusalemites have conflicting views about this subject. A thirty-year-old Arab social worker in East Jerusalem explained why he does not envision peace for many years.

"I think the Palestinians like myself will suffer more," he said. "I have no hope whatsoever of living a normal life. I never remember a day in my life when we had peace. All I remember is war and war, promises and insecurity. Not even one Arab in East Jerusalem is happy. How can you live under occupation and annexation? If I weren't married, I would have left for the States."

He sipped an orange juice and puffed on a cigarette.

"I don't believe in anybody who deals in politics. I'm just living day by day, and I don't know where I'm going. Many of my people in East Jerusalem have lost their sense of value as human beings. There is no Arab feeling of 'my country.' A rich Kuwaiti doesn't care if I live or die. I can see only one solution: if the Israelis will withdraw 100 percent from all lands taken in 1967. Of course, they won't."

An Israeli teacher, an intense, chain-smoking woman with tired eyes, looked at the situation differently.

"We Jews lost so many lives in the Yom Kippur War and sustained tragic injuries," she said. "Out of this vast Middle East we occupy a tiny piece of land. It is the homeland for us following the murder of six million Jews in the Holocaust. We have no other place in the world. While I yearn for peace in Jerusalem, I am not sure if it will come in my lifetime.

"Many of us sympathize with the Palestinian cause and seek a just solution to it. But we can't say that we are willing to be pushed into the sea. We must survive for the sake of millions of Jews who have perished as well as those who are still unborn. Will the Arabs allow us to survive in peace?"

Inside East Jerusalem the three great monotheistic religions intimately share holy places.

The primary places of spiritual and historical importance to Jews include the Western ("Wailing") Wall, a fragment of the ancient city wall that enclosed Solomon's Temple; the Tomb of David; and the cemetery stretching below the Mount of Olives. Israelis were denied access to these places during Arab occupation of East Jerusalem from 1948 to 1967.

The interlocking relationship between the holy places of the three faiths is striking. For example, the Dome of the Rock contains the rock on which Abraham was prepared to sacrifice Isaac. Jesus preached here and overturned the tables of the money changers. Mohammed ascended into the heavens from the Dome of the Rock. For Moslems, Jerusalem is the third-ranking holy place, following Mecca and Medina.

In East Jerusalem I chatted over tea with a Moslem whose family is an old and distinguished one in the city.

"Old Jerusalem has to return to the Moslems," he told me. "This is not only a political question. We're speaking of something belonging to a culture. If Islam is to be defeated over one of its holy places, one of two things will happen: first, an emnity will result between Moslems and Christians all over the world, and there will be international conflict—even if the Moslems have to spend every penny that they earn from oil until the oil wells are dry; or Islam may be destroyed, and the alternative for its six hundred million people will be to turn elsewhere—to atheism and Communism."

In 1852 Ottoman authorities, who then governed the city, reached an agreement with the different religious communities in Jerusalem defining their rights to specific holy places. Those arrangements continue to be operative today.

"If Jerusalem remains an undivided city and the capital of Israel, the government would not on principle be against entering into international obligations to guarantee the religious rights of all the concerned groups," an official of the Israel Foreign Office told me. "There are various legal possibilities for guaranteeing and maintaining the religious rights which the various communities now have."

Christian shrines in Jerusalem include the Church of the Holy Sepulchre, the scene of Jesus' Crucifixion at Golgotha; the Tomb of the Virgin Mary; and the Ascension Church atop the Mount of Olives. A fourth Christian shrine is the nearby Nativity Church in Bethlehem.

An Anglican bishop told me that perhaps there should be three protectors of East Jerusalem—the president of Israel, a Moslem monarch, and a Christian representative. However, Christians are sharply divided in Jerusalem, he explained, and would therefore be hard put to agree on the selection of a spokesman. Internationalization of the city has now generally been discredited as a solution by leaders of the three religions. Only continuation of free access to the holy places, as well as autonomous control of the sites, is considered essential.

The key to peace in Jerusalem can appear, on the surface, to be simply the question of sovereignty. This is deceptive. Peace rests far more deeply on the interaction of peoples. It has to be based on the subtle connections between vast social issues and small details of daily life, the pragmatic needs of Jerusalem's neighborhoods, and the ranging designs of world powers.

"The only city that may be compared to Jerusalem is Montreal," Mayor Teddy Kollek said. "There you have Frenchmen and Englishmen, and neither intends to become the other. Here we have no intention of making a goulash. Arabs will remain Arabs, and Jews, Jews. Neither wants assimilation. We do not wish to let the dividing lines vanish. You will find the same situation here in a hundred years. People want to stick to their roots. This is a positive and not a negative thing."

Americans are able to comprehend this situation because their traditional "melting pot" identification with "the American way of life" has recently come under sharp attack from many quarters. Ethnic and social groups in the United States now take a new pride in their differences, origins, and even varied aspirations. This has radically altered the makeup of American society.

In Jerusalem there is fear of "encroachment" on both sides. For example, a Jewish journalist told me, "Our danger lies in the Arabs' being so huge, so countless, so formless, and so immune to the usual dangers of the sophisticated nations. The persistent nuisance of Arab terror and threats and boycott might never stop harassing us."

A prominent Arab newspaper editor expressed another kind of fear: "The Israelis are trying to integrate us into their economy and social structure. They want to impose upon us their way of living."

Such conflicting viewpoints can seem to contribute to a crippling malaise. Yet a pattern—one that, I believe, holds out hope for peace—slowly emerges. Let's listen to what people who seek peace are saying.

One Arab spokesman, foreseeing a growth of rapport with Israelis as well as strong personal mutual involvement, went so far as to predict the emergence of a new Middle Eastern or Semitic culture that would combine the best of Jewish and Arab strains but place coexistence ahead of assimilation.

Pursuing a similar thought, a Jewish leader expressed hope when he also foresaw Jewish-Arab partnerships along social and economic lines. This would provide an increase in human contacts at staggered levels. He told me, "There's something in man that knows it's better to live together than kill each other."

"My dream is that there will be a trading federation for the Middle East, with Jerusalem as its capital," a Christian in East Jerusalem commented. "Everybody will have their rights in it. Israelis have the skills; Arabs, the people and markets. If Israel will be generous about the establishment of a Palestinian state, the Arabs might be generous about Jerusalem and entrust it to the Israelis."

Can there be peace in Jerusalem? My search in the Holy City for an answer led me to affirmative conclusions. I see numerous interlocking pieces of a jigsaw puzzle, pieces that can be handled sensitively and creatively in the interests of peace.

What are these pieces? They are small steps taken toward

a potential friend instead of the deadening traditional image of an enemy; men and women working together for common good instead of merely against each other; and slow, patient interaction between people mutually tired of war and destruction who yearn for peace.

Back in America, I found enormous complexity in the present situation involving Jews and Christians. Plain talk between them was difficult when they tried to discuss such specific subjects as Israel, the Third World, the Holocaust, or even their respective religious beliefs.

"My ancestry is Italian," a San Francisco businessman, a churchgoing Catholic, told me. "I have no right to involve America in Italian affairs and even risk war for the sake of defending Italy. Why do Jews think they have the right to involve America in Israel? If they want to give some of their own money to Israel, that's OK. But they have no right to make the rest of us contribute to Israel or risk war for its sake."

At the University of Michigan, a Jewish graduate student explained what Israel meant to him.

"I am not religious, but I see Israel as the Jewish homeland described in the Bible," he said. "Genocide awaits Jews. Look at the anti-Semitism, the utterly irrational hatred of Jews that is expressed in Christianity and so many parts of society. It leaps out unexpectedly all the time.

"The sole hope of escaping genocide for the world's Jews is the existence and health of the State of Israel. Maybe Jews will all become assimilated in the future; everybody may become the same. I don't know. But now, in this instant, Israel is the most important fact in the world for me as a Jew."

I chatted with a southern white Protestant clergyman who had been jailed in civil rights protests during the '60s.

"Don't we care about the Third World?" the clergyman asked. "How can we turn against our black brothers who support the Arabs and feel solidarity with the whole of the Third World and against Israel?"

Are blacks opposed to Israel?

"It would be sweeping the truth under a rug to say that there is not very widespread anti-semitism among blacks," said a young black journalist in the midwest. "But Jews marched with blacks and some shed their blood in our freedom struggle. My God, Jews are closer to blacks than Arabs who sold us into slavery. The Third World is something else. But there's an irony to consider. Even as an ally of America, isn't Israel closer to the poverty of the Third World than an oil-rich sheik in an American Cadillac? It's not an easy thing to figure."

A black social worker in Boston commented, "I was too young to know about the Holocaust, the Nazi era, and the suffering of Jews at that time. I have learned something about it from movies and TV. It pains me, sometimes unbearably, because I can see intersecting lines with black suffering and pain. I wept during a documentary about Jewish persecution under the Nazis. I have long been too occupied with the question of black freedom to have been conscious also of the Jewish experience. But now I begin to perceive it, and to sense what Israel means to Jews in terms of liberation and deliverance."

At the interfaith level, what did I find concerning the feelings of U.S. Christians and Jews toward each other?

"I *worry* about Jews," said a middle-aged white Christian woman during an interfaith discussion attended by a number of Christians and Jews in a suburb of Los Angeles. "My minister says they are going to hell because salvation is only through Jesus Christ."

"What we have in common at the deepest level as Jews and Christians is Jesus," said a Conservative rabbi in Cleveland. "I think about this particularly at Christmas.

For he stands between us. To me, he is one of us. You see, we look at him, as Christians and Jews, completely differently."

In America, Christianity tends to remain a threatening monolith to Jews, while Judaism is an enigma to Christians. Jews and Christians relate to one another too much by means of imagery instead of human interaction; so the cross is raised, the Talmud quoted; the church and the synagogue coolly coexist in burgeoning suburbs; Passover, Yom Kippur, Easter, and Christmas are observed. Yet a door is too often closed upon actual knowledge or experience of one another.

A Christian layman, a white Protestant with a fundamentalist background, described how struck with awe he was when he entered a synagogue for the first time in his life—at the age of forty-five—and chatted with the first rabbi whom he had ever met. Indeed, he explained to me, he had never before known a Jew as an individual.

"I called my wife after visiting the synagogue, talking to Jews, and meeting the rabbi. I don't know what to say about it all. I'm sorry I missed the opportunity a lot earlier in my life. I've heard all the same lies about Jews and blacks ever since I was a child, from people who claimed to know all about them but never actually knew any Jews or blacks. I've had so many distortions taught me. It takes endless energy to unlearn them."

A Jew with whom I chatted in Atlanta saw a vast gulf between Jews and Christians and wanted it to remain that way.

"The myth that Jews and Christians have a great deal in common is false," he said. "From the outset we have had little or nothing in common. It is false to argue otherwise and absolutely wrong to speak of a common Judeo-Christian heritage."

The question of Jewish-Christian relations was affected when Father Daniel Berrigan, the Jesuit who had long sustained a prophetic and courageous Christian witness in the peace movement and had gone to prison for destroying draft records in his opposition to the Vietnam war, publicly criticized Israel.

If Father Berrigan had made his speech before Jews instead of Arabs, or perhaps used language that was less inflammatory, he might have contributed creatively to Jewish-Christian dialogue. But for an internationally known Jesuit to speak as he did, and at a time when the Vatican had not officially recognized the State of Israel, was to set off a major controversy.

"I do not wish to heap conflict upon conflict," Father Berrigan told the Association of Arab University Graduates on October 19, 1973. The text of his speech was published in *American Report*. He described Israel as "a criminal Jewish community," a "nightmare" that "manufactures human waste," and an imperialist nation which is "the creation of an elite of millionaires, generals, and entrepreneurs."

"The wandering Jew became the settler Jew, the settler ethos became the imperial adventure," Father Berrigan told the Arab audience.

Thirteen million Jews are still alive in the world today. Of these, nearly three million live in Israel, the Jewish homeland. The rest are scattered. It is, perhaps, natural that all Jews, remembering the death of six million brethren in the Holocaust, are extraordinarily sensitive concerning the question of Israel's security. But there is not an imperial adventure, as Father Berrigan could have learned if he had visited Israel. He had not done so when he made his speech.

Inside Israel I found a self-critical society. I encountered outspoken criticism of every facet of Israeli life, from Arab and Jew alike. I discovered an awareness among many Israelis as well as Palestinians that both people have legitimate, if competing, national claims.

When Father Berrigan spoke of the tragedy "that the

State of Israel should become the repository, and finally the tomb, of the Jewish soul," I thought of the words uttered by Abraham Heschel, the revered Jewish scholar and spokesman for peace:

"I did not enter on my own the city of Jerusalem. Streams of endless craving, clinging, dreaming, flowing day and night, midnights, years, decades, centuries, millenia, streams of tears, pledging, waiting—from all over the world, from all corners of the earth—carried us of this generation to the Wall. My ancestors could only dream of you—to my people in Auschwitz you were more remote than the moon, and I could touch your stones! Am I worthy? How shall I ever repay for these moments?"

Jewish renewal in the State of Israel is to be welcomed and supported by Christians, I believe. So is a homeland for the Palestinian people. These two realities go hand in hand; they are no longer seen by responsible people in Israel or the United States as standing in opposition to each other. Indeed, a dream of new life, freedom, and prosperity in the Middle East is shared, as we have seen, by growing numbers of Israelis and Palestinians, Jews and Arabs.

Father Berrigan erred, in my opinion, when he said, "The Jews arose from the Holocaust, a cause of universal joy; but the Jews arose like warriors, armed to the teeth." The arising of the Jews was not at all a cause of universal joy. Indeed, past Jewish experiences in this world of politics and religions—including cruel interaction with more than an occasional Catholic or Protestant anti-Semite—led Jews toward a new self-strength. Father Berrigan mistook a determination not to be sacrificed lamblike inside a gas chamber for imperialism.

But in this address before Arab graduate students he seems to hold a curious image of Jews—that they are properly destined for wandering and suffering. That they have historically wandered and suffered is part of the evidence of Christian anti-Semitism directed against Jews for the mythical reason of committing deicide. Do Christians who put Jews to the rack and fire now demand Jewish conformity to a Christian-imposed image of martyrdom, continued deprivation, and pain?

"The question of Israel goes back to the fundamental difference between Judaism and Christianity," Rabbi Richard G. Hirsch told me one day in Jerusalem. "The continued existence of the Jewish people in a Jewish state, represents a challenge which is almost impossible for a Christian world to accept. It's easier to explain to a Christian why Jews do not accept Jesus than why a Jewish state. Because Christianity came into the world to demonstrate that geography, land, people were unimportant; universal ideas were important. So the people who became the most anti-Israel were the most Christian in terms of their theology, except for the fundamentalists. The latter are literally messianic, while liberal theology believes that man has to do something about it.

"Along comes the Jewish state, which reactivates latent emotions. We're a people. This phenomenon runs counter to the image of the Jew as the universal man. This image provided the common ground for the liberal Christian and the Jew. The Holocaust taught us that the world accepted our belief but didn't accept Jews. The test of Christianity isn't how you accept Jewish belief but Jews."

In his speech Father Berrigan said that the persecutor is a poor critic whose history weighs on him. He implied a form of emotional blackmail when he asked: "How then shall the goy judge the suffering servant?"

Father Berrigan seemed to misread an essential quality in many contemporary Christians. For guilt is not the motivating factor that he seemingly found it to be. Instead, the affirmation of life is this factor. It is rooted in the awareness that human lives are interrelated. We have come to know for whom the bell tolls.

I have long respected Daniel Berrigan for many reasons.

Not the least of these is his vulnerable and strong human spirit. I do not consider him to be a personal or self-conscious anti-Semite. Yet the end result of much of what he has said about Israel might be construed—and indeed, used by the enemies of Jews—as theological and social anti-Semitism. This, in the context of dangerously explosive anti-Jewish and anti-Israel sentiments that made their way around the world.

For example, King Faisal of Saudi Arabia, as reported by Religious News Service, issued a classic anti-Semitic statement that reached millions of people. The Jews "deviated from the truths of Moses," according to King Faisal, and they "attempted to murder Jesus Christ because they do not want the directives of God to be achieved."

Religion need not build high and impenetrable walls between people. Instead, it can assert the universality of faith, hope, and love. While deeply respecting the uniqueness and variances of people, religion can remind us that we are essentially brethren living in the world under one God.

Those of us who believed in, and served, the imperatives of the peace movement revered the late Abraham Heschel as a holy man and a prophet. He sometimes marched with us; eloquently he spoke for us.

Dr. Herschel wrote these words concerning Jewish commitment to Israel:

> Intimate attachment to the land, waiting for the renewal of Jewish life in the land of Israel, is part of our integrity, an existential fact. Unique, *sui generis*, it lives in our hope, it abides in our hearts.
>
> It is a commitment we must not betray. Three thousand years of faithfulness cannot be wiped off.
>
> To abandon the land would make a mockery of all our longings, prayers, and commitments. To abandon the land would be to repudiate the Bible.

It is necessary to realize that the destiny of Israel may well be determined by people and policies in the United States. Such a determination will inevitably not rest in the hands of Jews alone, for the whole climate of public opinion would inevitably prove to be of profound significance. Christians in America need to understand the dynamics of Jewish feeling concerning Israel, and indeed the full spectrum of Jewish opinion concerning Zionism and Judaism. This is impossible unless there is vastly improved communication, at varied levels, between Christians and Jews.

"At an interfaith level, Jews and Christians are equally hypocritical," a Jewish woman in San Francisco stated. "In my opinion, this shows a fear of rocking the boat on deeply controversial issues. So an uneasy and potentially dangerous status quo is maintained at any cost. Most Jews and Christians would rather settle for shallow brotherhood-week superficiality, and walk around on eggshells with each other, than speak the truth and trust one another to receive it."

I believe that Jews and Christians in the United States have indeed settled for a status quo arrangement that is marked by mutual awareness rigidly held at surface levels and an absence of serious interaction. Ethnicity has rightly asserted itself in opposition to a melting pot experience; the thrust of present American opinion is toward a healthy respect for differences. Look beneath the smooth outer facade of *any* life, including your own, and you will surely find the pieces of a mosaic. However, the very nature of differences must be explored, intellectually and empathically, as a prerequisite for establishing a solid basis of respect. The human family comes closer in the intimacy of what *can* be shared.

How can Jews and Christians interact? By accepting and loving each other without making continual judgments that look backward. By being practicing Jews or Christians, and setting an example. A good Jew, simply by the witness of his or her life, strongly helps a Christian to act according to Christian precepts and values. A good Christian, simply by the witness of his or her life, strongly helps a Jew to act according to Jewish precepts and values. For each life points to the love and justice of one God.

When I spoke one Friday evening in a Reform synagogue, a member of the congregation came up to talk to me after the service.

"I want to make a public apology to you," he said. "I don't like or trust Gentiles. When I heard that you were speaking here, I didn't want to come to hear you. I am glad that I came, and I want to apologize to you in this public way."

His generosity was matched only by his faithful sense of what needed to be done by a practicing Jew in an interfaith situation. He set an example for others—Christians and Jews alike—to speak the truth in love. It is the repression of feelings and thoughts that festers. To be straightforward and open with other people, especially when one's conscience is informed by love, is one of the most healing forces in all the world.

A Jew in Detroit asked me, "Is anti-Semitism so basic to the Christian faith as to render Christian-Jewish dialogue meaningless or hopeless?"

He was saying something about his own previous experience with Christian individuals or institutions. I felt that his experience of a new Christian response to him had to start with myself. If I responded in openness and love, and he could readily perceive this, a past chain reaction might be broken. Communication is preferable to its absence. A constructive relationship is a stronger human link than alienation.

The experience of Vietnam, and its proliferation of accompanying tragedies that included My Lai and Kent State, have sorely probed the spirituality and morality of

America. In the wake of Vietnam lay Watergate. The strength of the Judeo-Christian heritage as a living force therefore becomes a matter of urgency.

It is an anomaly to speak of Christian without Jew. We share in the rudiments of faith, Holy Scripture, a family tradition comprising the most creative and familiar aspects of love-hate closeness, and common aspirations that include the holiness of God and human justice. Finding ever anew the miracle of the Judeo-Christian heritage is one of my commitments, a bread-and-butter issue of my life and faith.

II

Superchrist of a Superstate: Political Manipulation of Christian

The wind blows fiercely against the hot sun on a summer's day. I rest for a moment, seated by wildflowers beneath an ancient oak tree. Dachau: isn't it within shouting distance? Belfast's charred houses: aren't they just over that ridge? Images of pain and violence in many parts of the world are intercut in my consciousness: the Acropolis that stood mere city blocks away from torture chambers; war refugees; starving children; urban crime; suffering political prisoners; the movement of racial separation that perpetuates apartheid.

The earth does not seem to be a coolly distant gray-orange sphere that astronauts gazed upon from the moon. The bridges of one's own intellect are under fire. A deadly opponent of the human spirit threatens to seize possession of a strategic hill that lies directly behind one's eyes.

I wonder: How can one survive as a whole human being with hope and courage? How can one serve the cause of loving when the force of hate literally overpowers so much of life? One has been told that religion is dead, its trunkful of truths mere shopworn platitudes that have been buried by a bitter and scarred generation.

Yet the Talmud speaks to me about the quality of life that I earnestly seek: "He who destroys a single life, it is as if he destroys the entire world. He who saves a single life, it is as if he saves the entire world." So nobility and meaningful sacrifice and compassion remain parts of life. Then Jesus responds directly to my questions and thoughts.

> For I was hungry and you gave me no food.
> I was thirsty and you gave me no drink.
> I was a stranger and you did not welcome me.
> Naked and you did not clothe me.
> Sick and in prison and you did not visit me.

I *can* do something. I can contribute to changing the very quality of my own life wherever I find it wanting. *We* can contribute to changing the very quality of life around us wherever we find it wanting.

But is religion an opiate of the people that ever betrays us, or is it an unflinching force of overpowering truth that lifts us up and reminds us eternally that we have been created in the image of God—and have the salvific work of love yet to carry on in solidarity with others?

There is a brand of Christianity which tells the rest of the world that it awaits the Second Coming of Christ to solve pressing "social problems" such as hunger, starvation, war, racism, sexism, colonialism, grinding poverty, and the absence of equal opportunity. This brand of Christianity explains that it renders unto God what belongs to God, and renders unto Caesar what belongs to Caesar, and it remains uninvolved in the arena of social issues. It lies.

For it is, in fact, cohesively involved in social issues by its support of the status quo on which it is dependent. It is rewarded by privilege, tax exemptions, and deductible financial benefits, and that ineffable sort of prestige bestowed traditionally upon docile religion by seasoned manipulators of caesaro-papism—which means to say, the state using religion for its own purposes.

Docile religion, in turn, provides those well-trained clergy who publicly mouth lukewarm yet politically supportive caricatures of prayers at government ceremonies or public assemblies, who plead with a partisan god to let "our" side win its wars, who distort the gospel of Christ in mealymouthed sermons to the mighty in palace chapels and White House East Rooms.

All this would not be so dangerous were it not for today's sophisticated technology. But—with almost insuperable irony—technology brings the McLuhan prophecy full circle so that the medium is the message. Take, for example, a giant revivalist rally—the lonely crowd flaunting religious symbols, and in the distance a superstar performing under bright lights.

Computers, television amplifiers—every technological, promotional, and publicity device has been put to work. The staff members—those disciples of P. T. Barnum, the patron saint whom American religion is too snobbishly dishonest to canonize—use every gimmick to bring out a record crowd. The preacher holds forth on "the gospel," but the gospel he preaches is a message of power, authority, public relations, packaging, speed, glamour, celebrity, magic.

A true Orwellian scene. The revivalist is a figure as friendly and familiar as Mary Tyler Moore, Jim Nabors, or Johnny Carson on the TV set. The crowd is pleased. So it accepts exploitation, letting the preacher baptize the process as evangelism. The computer used for the mechanics of this last hurrah has been transformed into an antigospel force, the *deus ex machina* that swells the "gospel crowd."

We are into the numbers game. Even otherwise sane people have come to gauge the significance of U.S. denominations in terms of numbers. American Christianity decided that it must grow and grow and grow. It is a friendly green giant in clerical collar. Technology is a godsend; it can ensure that a religious event will be "unprecedented" and draw more people than any other previous event. But where did JEEEE-sus go? Where, amid the big names, glamour and self-oriented themes, is the hard gospel moral-prophetic content? The scandal of the gospel is banished by a focus on worldly success. The betrayal of Jesus Chirst is perpetrated in his own name even as his own words are read aloud.

Yes, American religion has "grown." But the environmental-energy crisis confronted us with the realization that sheer growth can be negative and self-defeating and can even lead to extinction. We were warned to revise our criteria for measuring the quality of life. Yet when the question of "success" came under nearly universal discussion, American Christianity offered little moral-spiritual leadership. All the fake energy pumped into it gave American Christianity an illusory high, for it could point to the tags and size classifications attached to it.

As if that weren't enough, American Christianity has apparently gone into the export business with a bad product, one whose identity is based on fake energy and sheer size. As noted in the *Los Angeles Times* of August 17, 1974, an estimated 1.3 million persons attended the opening night of the Explo 74 crusade being held in Seoul, Korea, "amidst an aura of political trials and an assassination." This gathering at the massive evangelistic rally sponsored by Campus Crusade for Christ, said the report, "exceeded the 1.1 million who attended the last day of evangelist Billy Graham's Korean crusade in June, 1973, at the same location."

Given the theological and historical ambiguities of the word "crusade," with specific reference to the bloody and anti-Semitic Crusades themselves, one wonders why it surfaces in contemporary Christian revivalism. However, it pays off as a handle for publicity and it draws crowds as honey draws flies.

The Korean attendance figures—so a Campus Crusade official at the organization's headquarters in San Bernardino, California, told the *Los Angeles Times*—were "based on police estimates."

Indeed. For the "massive evangelistic rally" took place in a police state. The rally opened one day after a military courtmartial in Seoul sentenced Roman Catholic Bishop Daniel Tji and the Reverend Park Hyung Kyn, a Presbyterian minister, to fifteen years in jail on charges of "aiding opponents of President Park and violating Park's decrees." The sentences brought to 122 the number convicted since January, 1974, under emergency decrees that have had the effect of banning any political opposition.

"There is no religious persecution—they are political problems," William Bright, president of the Campus Crusade for Christ, replied when he was asked by newsmen a month earlier in Lausanne to comment on the number of clergy arrests that had taken place. In fact, "there is more religious freedom in South Korea than there is in the United States."

Yet ten top Protestant leaders in South Korea had recently issued a joint statement demanding the restoration of democracy. Among the signers were the moderator of the Presbyterian Church of Korea, a Methodist bishop, and the president of the Korean Evangelical Church.

Mr. Bright's comment about "no religious persecution—they are political problems" sounded peculiarly similar to a comment made by the South Korean foreign minister, Kim Dong Jo, in Seoul on August 15, 1974. "We are not trying a bishop, you know," he said in reference to Roman Catholic Bishop Tji who had just been sentenced. "We are trying a

Korean, Tji Hak Sun," he added, giving the clergyman's full Korean name. The foreign minister told news correspondent Sam Jameson that there were no political prisoners in South Korea, and said he was confident that the United States would not cut military aid to his country.

U.S. press reports documented that torture of citizens had taken place in South Korea. One quoted William J. Butler, a New York attorney who said in a report he filed for Amnesty International on July 30, 1974, that Kim Chi Ha, the internationally known poet, "gave evidence of being tortured" when he appeared at his courtmartial. His mother was detained and beaten for three days from July 26 and was later detained by the police for a second time.

Lee Kwang Il, a twenty-four-year-old student at Han Kuk Theological Seminary and former president of the Korean Association of Church Youth, was sentenced to twenty years in jail. A press report from Seoul on August 23, 1974, said that his mother was detained by authorities "and was beaten unconscious." She was hospitalized after being released, the report said. A number of citizens, it was reported, were being detained and interrogated "about the leaks to the foreign press about torture of prisoners."

Crowds notwithstanding, the integrity of Christian witness was sharply called into question by the juxtaposition of authoritarian government permission for the "massive evangelical rally" on the one hand, and prison sentences meted out by that same government to Christians from whose religious and moral persecution the visiting U.S. revivalists apparently disassociated themselves, on the other.

One would like to ask why "there is more religious freedom in South Korea than there is in the United States." Religious freedom for whom? What gospel are we talking about? For those religionists whose silence on the gospel's justice and mercy wins them the goodwill of a police state, is "more religious freedom" measured, for example, in terms of a controlled press, crowd manipulation, and the imprimatur of Caesar?

Recently I made a journey across America. My purpose was to study the condition of America's soul. I listened to people, getting close to them, and tried to sense their feelings. Raw and sensitive needs were expressed in sometimes uncontrollable outpourings of feeling. But what was the response of organized religion to such chaotic need? I attended many different worship services and listened to a number of sermons in an effort to find out. However, these did not provide an answer.

For the worship generally remained rigid in form, unyieldingly traditional in content, and provided neither a sense of people's feelings nor an outlet for them. Sermons were almost without exception either "how-to" instructional directives concerning personal emotional problems, Bible-thumping "other-worldly" messages, or polite homilies—one was a minister's travelogue-account of a visit to historic places in Israel. Much of organized religion, as seen in its public worship, seemed studiedly to be avoiding a theological or an existential involvement in the social-cultural issues that represented the immediate spiritual context of most people's real lives.

Among a growing number of people I discovered that there is now a commonly accepted belief in some form of an encroaching universal doom. It may take the form of the death of a city, the destruction of a nation, or the end of human life. It may come from insoluble problems or inexorable forces within one's own environment rather than from any form of an enemy attack. A number of people told me that it may be linked indissolubly to mounting violence as a way of life.

Indeed, Stanley Kubrick's archetypal film *A Clockwork Orange* went so far as to depict modern worship of a god of violence. As ancient Aztecs tore human hearts from living bodies for a holy sacrifice, so the young men in the film ran with verve as they stomped a helpless old man, gang-raped a woman while kicking to a pulp the face of her watching husband, and crushed the skull of another woman.

This worship of a god is passionate, self-immolating, taut with commitment. These extremely devout youths are absolutely caught up in the liturgies and rites of worshiping their deity.

I must observe that such adherence to a creed represents far more profound communion with a god than the lukewarm, lifeless travesty of worship that is to be found in countless piously conventional Christian churches. It seems to me that the god of violence is honored and loved more in American society than is the God of love and peace. Casual acceptance of such violence means that our humanity is seriously threatened. Writing in *The Day of the Locust*, Nathanael West warned that people consumed by the fury of an "awful, anarchic power . . . had it in them to destroy civilization."

I turned to individuals in the religious community, asking them about the condition of America's soul.

A rabbi in New York reported that he found a desperate yearning to believe on the part of the people.

"People are saying 'Give me faith.' Yet along with this is a gnawing awareness of realities, anxiety, and disgust. The bombing in Cambodia went on and on. America lacks compassion for other people and it puts material things first, choking its soul. The Watergate guys played cops and robbers with this country. We've been assaulted and raped every day. 'It can't happen here' used to be our claim. Well, it *has* happened. Everybody used to say this was the greatest country in the world. Nobody can say that with a straight face now. There used to be such a hubris and pride. Now it's a question about our integrity instead. We're no purer than anybody else. My deepest spiritual reaction is that I'm furious."

A minister's wife pondered the dilemma of what an individual could do in order to effect social change or find personal fulfillment.

"I went to jail for civil rights and against the war in Vietnam," she explained. "I think I was doing something to let the problem be known. But that time has gone forever. Now I don't have any idea about either what time has come or what I can do."

A nun in California, a teacher in a parochial school, had observed her twenty-fifth anniversary of religious service on the day I spoke with her.

"America's soul? It's a melting pot of the feelings, cares, and understandings of diverse people who came here," she said. "This soul has to express itself. All the anger, dirt, and frustrations need to come out. After that, there can be a new beginning. Underneath the surface, people are saying 'You don't really care about me. You can't actually understand because you don't feel as I feel.' In order to care, one has to have some deep empathy. In order to love, one must hold oneself wide open to other people. Yet people merely pretend to communicate. Instead they are insensitive, deeply troubled, searching for their real self. Insecurity is the great overtone."

She stood up and walked around the room. "So it is a time of great challenge. Yes, I'm tired, in a sense, because it is difficult to hold standards and maintain an ideal when ideals are considered obsolete. We have a tremendous need for renewal—in business, in religion, in government. Patterns for the future cannot use an old map. Instead we need to break down old forms and restructure. We need a new set of pioneers."

In conversations with a cross section of people—mechanics and housewives, lawyers and students, office workers and teachers—I heard expressions of fear, cynicism, dismay, hurt, incredulity, frustration, enthusiasm, anger, mistrust, hope, fatigue, sadness, confidence, alienation, fury.

A former Roman Catholic priest, living with his wife and children in Minnesota, told me that he frankly did not know if people any longer possess the power to bring about changes in society. "I'm trying to hang in and work for social change and betterment. But if there's no reinforcement, if it doesn't really matter whether you make an effort or not, then I'm going to become a bartender and drop out of the fight."

Although the American mood was dissonant, often perverse and malignant, nevertheless it seemed to burgeon with mixed challenges and hopes. I found a contradiction between a buoyant determination to take control of destiny and a brooding malaise rooted in the fear that it might now be out of control. The contradiction could be found within one and the same person.

Take, for example, a sensitive, exceptionally well-informed and profoundly concerned man—a man who, in fact, is a central figure in contemporary American journalism. We sat in his house one night, chatting into the small hours.

He had a melancholy foreboding, he confessed, that a future presidential election would be sabotaged and not held; that police-state repression would be visited upon known and marked critics in opposition in America, as it had been in a number of foreign countries. Yet a bit later in our conversation he optimistically spoke in precise detail of his plans and efforts for achieving political and social changes within his local community as well as on a national level. They were hopeful and highly energetic efforts, shared in solidarity with colleagues and opened up for mass examination by means of publicity.

A black graduate student from Alabama, enrolled in a school of social work, looked at me through his glasses. "I'm trying to evaluate what is happening. I'm very much into school. I'm working hard. All I'm trying to do is get someplace where I can have something. But I find myself asking: Am I hustling for nothing? Confronting the situation as it is, and seems to be going, I try not to look closely at it. The system is so corrupt and rotten. Who is honest? Who is telling the truth about anything? I can't see how there will be any way for a man to be successful without selling his soul."

A woman who is a lawyer in Los Angeles viewed the situation quite differently.

"I feel unholy glee," she said, laughing. "I feel as if there has been an unveiling—not just an uncovering. The whole rotten mess is open to public view. It's like the prophetic things of old. 'See no evil.' A rabbi was talking about Jeremiah and Watergate last Friday night at the temple. I don't know who the prophets are right now. But somehow the drive and the forces are here to get our problems out of the underground. It's what the kids, the liberals, the blacks had tried to do for so long. Now there needs to be a pulling together of forces."

An artist employed in Hollywood scoffed at the idea of moral cleansing.

"The idea of a purge or cleansing is like witch-burning," she said. "The zealots do harm that they don't understand. They used to hold the flag up so high and say that Americans could do no wrong. Now the new fellows playing the good guys are coming up, striving for power. They'll get smeared, too."

She laughed. "My God, you get a claustrophobic feeling. Denseness. Heaviness. I'm tired. I'd like to run away and I can't. I can't find anything."

A retired dentist described himself as an optimist.

"When 'The Star-Spangled Banner' is played, I get a lump in my throat. But I don't see young people feeling that way. I don't think they'd fight for the country if they had to. I don't see them breaking their neck for their country. I was in the navy when Roosevelt died. Tears came to my eyes, more than when my father died. I am one of those real loyal Americans who loves his country. I've been a Democrat all my life. I voted Republican the first time for Nixon."

He drank a gin and tonic as he talked.

"I never had a feeling of love for Nixon. He was too aloof or something. You couldn't get a kindly vibration toward him. This country needs a great leader now. A man whom we could say about, 'This is our man.' However, I remember during the Depression when Hoover was booed. I thought 'You bastards. That's the president.' Oh, I'm hurt. That people in government would do this to us and to themselves. Honesty has to be a basic in life."

A black teacher in a Midwest junior high school echoed this expression of personal pain. "It's like an explosion inside of me. When I see people explaining away the whole system of justice that I grew up respecting, it says to me this could be the beginning of the end. I feel deep moral fatigue because of my inability to find small rays of hope. The system of violence seems to underlie everything. The crises come and go with such force and rapidity that you can't be very upset. You just wait around for the next one."

A white teacher of first-grade children shared this fear. "Our society is so hollow in its moral resources. I'm fearful that we don't have the capacity to do what is needed. We operate on one another the way the Watergate conspirators acted on one another."

She expressed a sense of frustration.

"I'm trying to find a purpose for my own activities. I want to do something useful. But the school system doesn't really want to deal with the child. The child is supposed to accommodate to the school. And so many older kids think they're protesting, but they have no values. The kids themselves have no control over the forces that are shaping them."

Bill, an eighteen-year-old suburban high school student, discussed this problem. "I remember watching TV, and McGovern was predicting everything that happened under Nixon. You always hear that twenty years ago America was supposed to be so great. Now it seems like it's all kind of slipped and gone down the tube. America is a whole mess of stuff. There are people who care and give. There are others who won't. Mostly I find that nobody is together with anybody else. It's live for yourself."

How did he manage in this situation?

"It's kind of hard. Somebody who you think might be a good friend tries to rip you off. In my school there's no communication. Everyone has his own little social group. Jocks. Hippies. Musicians. Smart students. Barriers are never broken. You can't just walk up to someone and talk to him and say hi. I don't know anybody black because there aren't any of them around."

Was he hopeful about his future?

"I'm trying. If I can make it, well, I'm giving it a chance."

Did the people with whom I talked believe that they possessed the power to affect changes in the society?

A nutritionist employed in a Detroit hospital spoke of "having no control" over events and forces within society.

"I'm trying not to think about fear," she said. "What are we going to do? The whole society seems to be just bobbling. Everything is unstable. We don't know who's lying. You get tired of hearing the same thing and don't know who's telling the truth. We're just not getting anyplace. I'm wrung out mentally and spiritually."

A black psychiatrist spoke of moral fatigue. "I feel both

fear and pity for this country. Some people are morally tired out and don't know how fragmented their individual rights already are. I understand that my freedom is at stake. The whole control and surveillance mechanism is awesome."

Did other people seek an emerging leader?

"I stopped looking for a leader sometime back," said a community organizer in New England. "But sadly that leaves a vacuum of powerlessness, doesn't it?

In Chicago, a teacher working with teen-age delinquents spoke critically of the leaders accepted by these youths.

"These kids are cynical and searching," he said. "Some of my hardest struggles are to get them to accept the seriousness of the age. But instead they like media celebrities and movement hoodlums. The kids are looking at these guys who are outdated and they say, 'This is the way it should be. Right on!' It's very sad."

A TV producer in San Francisco commented: "I want a leader who's honest. Period. To hell with Democrat or Republican. I don't care what label a guy wears."

A black college official told me, "There is no moral leadership. There is no sense of anyone's caring strongly, loving deeply, or trying to turn around a near-hopeless racial situation. The inner cities are black, the suburbs white. There are few bridges or lines of communication between them. A match could ignite an inferno that would make Washington, D.C., after Martin Luther King's murder look like child's play. And nobody—nobody—is doing a damned thing to stop it. America's soul is in deep trouble."

Where might I find a new set of pioneers? If patterns for the future could not use an old map, I would look for a sign of renewal in a community that had undergone destruction. I visited Watts, the Los Angeles ghetto that erupted in fiery revolt in mid-August 1965, an event that cost more than thirty lives and turned city streets into ruins.

"That Moynihan guy was the modern Machiavelli when

he told the modern prince, Richard Nixon, to use benign neglect as his way with America's black people," a black social worker told me. We were chatting over beer and Fritos inside his house in Watts. "The prince took his advice. Benign neglect is what you see today in Watts and in most of the country's inner cities. They're dying. Watts is a lot worse off now than before the revolt. There are street gangs now, blacks killing blacks. Nobody on the outside cares when whites aren't being killed. Me, I used to be a militant. I'm harmless now—an animal the system has changed into an educated, middle-class black man."

Nearly a decade after the 1965 revolt, I was back in the streets of Watts. I wanted to find out what the people there had to say about America's soul. The first member of the community I talked to was a young black man wearing blue jeans, a Levi jacket, and a black leather flop hat.

"Where are we today? Really just in 1955," he said. "We have been in a period of regression, one of gangs and games."

"How come?" I asked him.

"Two things are missing," he answered. "First, a sense of self-determination. People ask for things but lack the will to go ahead and do for themselves. Second, a value system. We've got to have it if we're going to deal realistically with any kind of power. Or else a black man with a gun is as likely to shoot me as to shoot a white boy."

In broad daylight beneath a burning sun, Watts resembled a ghost town despite the fact that men, women, and children walked along its streets. Empty lots loomed where shops once stood. Many houses and stores were boarded up.

Two years before, signs along 103 Street indicated who was still in business: "Wigs—restyled $3.50 Up"; "Auto Insurance—Monthly Payments"; "Notary Public—Income Tax"; "Live Poultry, Fresh Fish." Here, a storefront church was a going concern. Over there, the fashion "House of Uhru" was already dead; "Black Egyptians" was scrawled on its wall. "Get on the Soul Express" was painted on a bus-stop street bench where a middle-aged man sat staring vacantly at the scene. "God Is the Sun" was scribbled on the wall of a nearby store.

Today Watts was deader than a doornail. Those signs were gone, and so were the businesses they fronted for. Social agencies were still here; indeed, one of them was going to erect an expensive new building. ("Hopefully it will make money for a black architect and black workers," a Watts resident told me.) Low-income housing was under construction—it was reported to be too expensive for low-income people. Watts looked like, felt like, a ghost town.

"This *is* a ghost town," an intense, attractive young black woman said. "If you scatter people widely enough, you make sure they've got a squeak instead of a voice. There isn't a united voice here anymore because the concentration has been broken up. Next the city plans to build two-story townhouses, a shopping mall, and underground passage-ways. It will be expensive. And it will be an entirely different community. Whites can afford it, and maybe some middle-class, achieving blacks will move back here. What they want is to remove a scar, a blemish from the city. They don't care about the people at all. They'll make a new image."

But why did the city permit the annual Watts summer festival?

"Because it keeps the people occupied," she replied. "Then they can't make trouble. The city shows the rest of the world, 'These people are happy. Look at them.' "

"But," she added, "don't use my name in anything you write." She was employed by the city of Los Angeles to work with people in the Watts community, she said, and "I can't afford to shake up the people who hire me until I really get my foot in the door."

An elderly black woman I talked to on the street was pessimistic: "In Detroit, when they moved people out of what was known as Black Bottom, new people moved in with rents starting at $125. The same thing will happen here. They'll try to change the name when they can without the people protesting. Maybe they'll call it 'Watts Heights.' "

I had been in these Watts ghetto streets during the 1965 revolt, listening to people's words, trying to understand what triggered the violence. I remember standing on a street strewn with shattered glass and shadowed by the shells of fire-gutted buildings. A crowd had gathered; voices were raised.

"The reason people are throwing rocks and burning stores isn't for a free bottle of whiskey or a dress," a man said. "People are tired, tired, tired."

"Pretty soon I'll be thirty," a black woman announced. "I don't want to sweep floors all of my life."

"If we follow the road of nonviolence, we'll never get rid of the man," remarked a black youth. "We're going to have to have some show of force. Some of this must be economic and political. But basically it's got to be just sheer force."

Soldiers stood close by, rigidly holding their guns. A black woman pointed toward them and said: "A white cop stopped my car to give me a ticket the other day. He just stood there and said, 'Get out, nigger bitch.' I'm not going to take that any more from the blue-eyed devil."

A uniformed national guardsman walked over to where we all stood on the street and ordered us to disperse. I walked away with a young black. He had not finished high school, he told me. "The man has always been killing. He first drove the Indians out. Now *my* arm's almost been bit off. I've got to bite back. There'll be more riots until the man opens his eyes and says, 'We're going to give it to you because we're tired.' "

"Every day of the riots is worth a year of civil rights demonstrations," a young black militant said. "I knew this would happen. I looked forward to it."

That was Watts in mid-August, 1965. In 1972 I visited an exhibit of black art at the Watts Summer Festival. A crowd made up of white visitors and Watts residents milled around the exhibit area, looking at the display.

"It's so damn stylized," commented one white. "There's nothing out of pain." No? Nearby was a painting showing a lacerated black man lying dead on a bloodstained bed while twenty pairs of eyes gazed at him. It was entitled *Systematic Genocide or Justified Homicide*. Next to this hung *Watts Riot End of World?* which depicted a gigantic explosion, flaming red.

"Maybe Watts exists only in a white image now," commented another white visitor to the exhibit. "The black people are really ashamed of what happened in 1965 and are trying to hide it, put it down."

So? I noted the painting of a black youngster who was simultaneously trying to hide his face and to look at life outside. I noted *Quiet Room*, a black woman, markedly disturbed, sitting naked and alone. And I noted *I've Got Rhythm*, an art object made up of a metronome with a photograph of a lynch mob pasted on it, a tiny hanging black figure, a miniature American flag, and a crucifix.

Of course the stereotype Aunt Jemima appeared in some of the paintings, Angela Davis was on hand in both oils and photographs, and black Jesuses abounded. But many of the pictures showed old and young black people crying.

Self-Portrait powerfully revealed the face of a young man with pain in his eyes. *Summer Vacation* depicted a teen-age youth hemmed in by tree branches, steel spikes, fire, and a wall. The mythology of Watts was represented by a few Shaft-like portrayals of angry young black men holding guns. *Been Down So Long It Looks Like Up* was a wooden art object containing a U.S. flag and a mousetrap that hung from the ceiling.

Super Black showed a black youth attired in a Superman outfit decorated with buttons that read "War Hero," "Yale," "Actor," "L.A. Rams," and so on. Printed beneath the portrait were the words: "Super Black came from across the tracks. Now he says he is not going back. . . . Mom's at home crying aloud wondering where is the child who is standing proud. He's been accepted."

Outside the exhibit area in Will Rogers Park, a number of U.S. military recruitment posters and photographs of top black brass were on display. Three black servicemen sat at a table. "Maybe they'll trot out their black admiral," someone remarked.

Was Watts supposed to prove that riots don't pay?

"Blacks want Watts torn down," a white community organizer told me. "They see how, in some respects, it's a blight in their minds. One guy who used to work here said the only thing that needs to be done with Watts is putting a bulldozer through it. You see, the old defiant Watts rhetoric seemed to make sense when there was a Kennedy or a Johnson administration and a belief that you could say those words and gain something from it. Now there's a fear that if you push rhetoric too far and do anything to back it up, you might get badly hurt."

I chatted with a young black militant.

"Church or summer festival is the only way to draw a great crowd of black people," he said. "The church makes Jesus black, puts a bandana on him, makes him a revolutionary, and says 'Thou shalt not kill.' It's hip if you can make it."

I asked him: Where does the black revolution go from here?

"Most revolutionaries or potential revolutionaries are on the campuses. The elitists and bourgeoisie, in conjunction with the people, make the revolution. But these cats come out here and quote Fanon, Mao, Che, Castro, Nkrumah—everybody. I can't remember any of it. Necessity will force them back to where the people are. Eric Hoffer says a movement can succeed without a god but needs a devil. The white boy will be the devil—like Hitler. Hitler became the unifying force and brought about unity."

But at what cost? Six million Jews lost their lives.

"Freedom is not free," the militant replied. "I hope blacks won't have to pay that kind of price. However, I don't think America will let us pay less."

A car drives along the street bearing this bumper sticker: "Good neighbors come in all colors."

What revolutionary strategy, I asked, seems possible?

"The Jews have Israel," the militant said. "We've got to have some place to come *from*. We're almost extinct culturally, but they can't destroy us as people. Nationalists have got to begin to do the work of establishing nationalism with black people in America. You've got to be where the people are at."

As I listened to the residents of Watts, even as I heard many other people in a wide cross section of American men and women, it occurred to me that seldom had there been such an urgent need in our nation's life for moral guidance and spiritual assistance. Yet institutional morality and spirituality are sorely hindered today. They are publicly represented by an authority that is itself under question and that many argue is isolated from people and realities, locked away in inflexible structures, dehumanizing rules and bureaucratic patterns.

We want comfort. Does God give us comfort? We want peace. Does God give us peace? No. Not in any privatized, self-serving way in the midst of an agonized world. Organized religion is largely to blame for our misconceptions about these considerations. It wanted to keep its doors open and thought that telling us what we wanted to hear might at least meet that objective.

Nonetheless we have been misinformed, promised a rose garden, and led down the primrose path. We realize it now.

Each of us, in one way or another, is engaged in a small pilgrimage toward truth, fulfillment, meaning, responsibility, joy—God. I believe that now we must get these small pilgrimages together and share the big one. It must include an involved, pragmatic concern about meeting the planet's problems and one's own personal concerns. Christianity, when it is practiced, gives us the answer to both. It doesn't offer us a personal gospel here and a social gospel there. It offers only the gospel that combines the personal and the social.

Clearly, we haven't accepted Christ either personally or socially, and the result can be found in the wreckage that surrounds us. But this is our failure, and Christ points the way for us to overcome it. He offers us communion with God and then each other. Christ wants us to come freely to him. He respects our God-given free wills, never wishing to manipulate us.

America's soul is troubled. People feel guilty, frustrated, and restlessly anxious. The gap between people's unfilled spiritual needs and organized religion's failure of nerve is soil for a demagogic, chauvinistic national religious movement. And this, I believe, is one of the most frightening prospects Americans will come upon in the future if steps to prevent it are not taken now. I speak of "melting pot" religion, with conformity built in and the most rigid doctrinal allegiance enforced.

"Do you accept Jesus Christ as your personal Lord and Savior?" would be the inquisitorial question asked. There would be no counter-question, definition of language, or dialogue. "Answer yes or no."

Technology innocently moves us ever closer to a computer-structured organization of religion. People's requests for information or help—"What is the Trinity?" "How can I remain faithful to my wife?"—are fed into computers which answer by printed forms. Mass questions get mass replies.

Add patriotism. At first subtly, then quite obviously, add patriotism to religion as a prime good of the nation. Then a mass-structured organization can more openly take on a quasi-military form. The leaders of the religion can address the masses of people, whether in great arenas or via TV, in their own living rooms—for at this stage blocks of TV time will be available to religion. Thus vastly popular and celebrated public figures, the leaders of religion, themselves can now be identified as colleagues and friends of the heads of state. So church and state move closer and closer together.

In the early '70s, tyranny came dangerously close. Government surveillance of private citizens was unprecedented in scope. The people were not even informed of their government's bombing of a foreign country. Government agencies were harassed to be at the disposal of the executive branch for immoral and illegal actions taken against citizens. There were "enemy lists" of citizens.

At the same time, the weight of public religion was long under-critical of the government—long after reasoned voices of dissent has been raised within the Christian body. Finally it objected not so much to actions or motives but to "bad language" on tapes. It was generally supportive, in fact, of a racist, militaristic, morally unprincipled administration that malevolently posed in religious trappings, sponsored White House prayer services, and piously appeared at "prayer breakfasts"—when people bowed their heads in unison for photographers, even as they knew that bombs were falling on other heads of innocent people and the poor were being betrayed at home.

Billy Graham, the revivalist, became the religious symbol of spirituality. It was Mr. Graham who once seemed to be a

White House chaplain-at-large. The Gallup Poll has reported Mr. Graham on its annual listing of Americans most admired in the world. In 1972 and 1973, he shared top billing on the "top ten" list with Richard M. Nixon. From the standpoint of sheer worldly power and a worldwide capacity for public relations, Mr. Graham's views and positions had come to assume significance not only for his own followers but for millions of other people as well.

In the fall of 1973 I asked a prominent U.S. newspaper editor why the nation's press had seemingly treated Graham as sacrosanct, somehow above the level of criticism reserved for politicians, movie stars, athletes, and less exalted Christian critics of the Nixon administration.

He responded: "Graham is the American apotheosis of virtue. He *is* religion, yet it is so partial and limited. One looks in vain for the element of significant sacrifice."

Upon taking office as President, Gerald Ford announced to the American people that the recent political nightmare was over. I concurred in his hope. But I knew that we needed to learn lessons from it that might save us from any future tyranny when a superchurch could be a prayerful, uncritical, "God-representing" and antiprophetic adjunct of a superstate, with a superchrist on a convenient altar.

Mr. Graham was no doubt innocent of any conscious wrongdoing when the two public figures of Billy Graham and Richard Nixon drew close. Presumably he felt that he acted in the public good and, certainly, God's good. Yet when these two figures moved still closer together in the public eye and the national consciousness, church and state veered closer than they were ever meant to do.

As a key figure in a caesaro-papist mosaic, Billy Graham could perhaps not have been expected to say very much about the Watergate scandal.

On May 6, 1973, the revivalist acknowledged that Watergate was "sordid," but he warned of "newspaper and television headlines based on rumors," and commented, "Let's face it—we need supernatural help!"

Mr. Graham revealed where he stood on Watergate in a short article he wrote for the op-ed page of the *New York Times*. He asked: "What can we do? Where can we turn? Is it too late?" Then he offered four suggestions of positive action that could be taken.

First, he said, "We need a national and pervasive awakening that includes repentance for our individual and corporate sins."

Yet when did Mr. Graham publicly confess the corporate sins of My Lai, Attica, Kent State, Jackson State, the tiger cages, and Bach Mai? These highly specific sins long needed to be repented.

Second, he said, "We must put the Watergate affair in proper historical perspective. America has lived through many moral political crises. . . No political party can claim the title of 'Mr. Clean.' "

The Fair Campaign Practices Committee was far more prophetic than Mr. Graham, from a biblical and theological standpoint, when it stated on May 27, 1973, that it "has uncovered no campaign tactics comparable in extent or in potential damage to a free, self-governing society" in its existence. The committee checked the facts and then spoke openly and courageously about what it had found.

The private, nonpartisan group elaborated, "The sordid scandal called the Watergate affair is not simply more of the same tactics which have made 'politics' a dirty word. It is a conscious conspiracy to violate laws, to manipulate voters, and to make a mockery of the democratic system of self-government."

Third, Mr. Graham said, "The media—including press, radio and television—that have opened up the Watergate issue can almost make us do, buy, sell or think any way they wish. They could render constructive service to the nation at this critical moment of history if they joined hands with the churches and synagogues and used their vast powers to fan the dying embers of the moral and spiritual life of the nation."

Mr. Graham did not seem to understand that the moral and spiritual life of the nation is not enclosed within the Establishment walls of churches and synagogues, many of which remained as silent as he did concerning the immorality of the Indochina war; listen to Bible readings for one hour a week but practice racism; and engage in spending millions of dollars for new buildings while people remain hungry and some starve to death.

In any event, the institutions that outwardly represent the Judeo-Christian tradition would surely not wish to "use" the mass media in order to exploit or manipulate people for "moral and spiritual" purposes. But these media were already fanning "the dying embers of the moral and spiritual life of the nation" by exposing Watergate.

Lastly, Mr. Graham pointed out, "Perhaps Watergate can teach us that we need to take the law of Moses and the Sermon on the Mount seriously. . . . The moral laws expressed in these two great documents could form the moral guidelines for every American."

What has made people turn away from traditional moral laws? The hypocrisy of White House worship services—where the prayers were ostensibly as carefully screened as the people present—and revivalistic rallies—placing an almost masturbatory emphasis on personal sins while comfortably glossing over the corporate sins of an aggressive, often imperialistic America—have negated moral laws that went publicly unpracticed as well as great spiritual documents that were contradicted in life.

Mr. Graham must know that God is not a deus ex machina to be employed for a quick miracle that could clean up—presto!—an ungodly mess of conflicting lies. One wonders why Mr. Graham did not speak about Watergate during the many months when it first dominated the nation's headlines. One wonders, too, why Mr. Graham did not speak in a profoundly spiritual and incisive way to his friend the president about it.

Mr. Graham said that he found the Watergate scandal to be a symptom of the "permissiveness, corruption and crime" permeating much of American life. But this remark followed his long silence during the Indochina war. Why didn't Mr. Graham earlier excoriate the "permissiveness" of bombing civilians and destroying a land, the "corruption" inside the character of men surrounding the U.S. president, and the "crime" of treating America's minorities with benign neglect while spending a fortune to destroy Vietnam in order to save it?

Mr. Graham has long held access to U.S. presidents. Other religious spokesmen who held opposing views were denied equal access to Richard M. Nixon. Mr. Graham did not intervene to break the president's isolation from ideas, including moral and religious ones, that differed from those held by the people tightly surrounding him.

President Nixon seemingly sought to bridge the division between church and state in an assiduously promoted association with Mr. Graham, who accepted the prestige and publicity that accompany a walk in the corridors of power. The public remembers when Mr. Nixon joined twelve thousand residents of Charlotte, North Carolina, to honor Mr. Graham, and when the revivalist acted as co-chairman with Bob Hope for "Honor America Day" in Washington, D.C.

Writing about Mr. Nixon's victory in *The Selling of the President 1968*, Joe McGinniss recalls Mr. Graham's entrance into the president-elect's New York hotel suite. " 'We did it,' he said, grinning, his blond hair neatly waved. He went directly to Nixon's room, without explaining whether 'we' meant Billy Graham and Richard Nixon or Billy Graham and God or perhaps all three together."

In his first televised "Watergate message" to the nation, President Nixon asked for the people's prayers. What did he mean? Prayers are not messages in gothic English addressed to a figure with a beard who inhabits the sky. Men and women are co-creators with God in the continuing and responsible act of creation. So prayers comprise actions even more than words. Therefore, honest dissent and constructive criticism, coming from the consciences of sensitive men and women, were possibly the finest prayer that one could offer for the president. Yet the Nixon administration—one sadly wonders to what extent this may implicitly have included Mr. Graham—never understood that principled dissent is a form of prayer for America.

"God Bless America," Mr. Nixon said at the conclusion of that same message. One must ask if he knew that God does not bless America any more than Cambodia, Brazil, the Vietnams, France and Nigeria.

The Nixon administration, with Mr. Graham cast frequently as one of its superstars, conspicuously engaged in public relations–engineered religiosity. Any attempt to establish in people's minds a belief in a nondissenting, conformist, civil religion approaches gross blasphemy. Getting down to the nitty-gritty God business of practicing integrity in political ethics and decency in treatment of the poor and dispossessed would surely serve God far better.

There were other religious characters in the Watergate morality play. These included Father John McLaughlin, Rabbi Baruch Korff, and the Reverend Sun Myung Moon, who came to the United States from the military dictatorship of South Korea which jailed and tortured Christians who opposed its tyranny, while it rewarded with government friendship Christian "evangelists" who did not criticize its abridgments of human rights or raise a finger to help their Christian brethren in chains.

But Rabbi Korff and the Reverend Messrs. McLaughlin and Moon were never superstars of the morality play; rather, they were fascinating cameo players. Billy Graham was the superstar. He must surely be considered a religious leader, but it is a serious question now to what extent he has compromised his position as a moral leader.

I went to St. Paul, Minnesota, on July 16, 1973, to attend "Youth Night" at the Billy Graham Upper Midwest Crusade that was being held there. Graham epitomized the pinnacle of present-day American religious revivalism when he appeared that night at the Minnesota State Fairgrounds. He brought out a crowd of thousands.

I watched Billy Graham closely that night. As I did so, I recalled a long-forgotten visit I had made to a mass meeting that the revivalist had held in the mid-1950s in Madison Square Garden. After its conclusion I walked the empty New York City streets past midnight. I felt unease and was beset by troubling questions.

Was this evangelism? But how was Jesus' bloody cross linked to the instant success of statistical conversions? Was salvation only a personal matter? But what about racism, war, and poverty? I didn't find the spirit of worship at the cut-and-dried, professionally organized, and publicity engendered mass worship. There was a lack of a sense of the holy, of sensitivity. I felt no awareness of personal identity or community or God.

Now, here in the vast throng was Billy Graham. He was folksy as he spoke to the crowd. He told of his innocence with an early girl friend when he was a youth. "It was puppy love but it was real to the puppy." He warned against drugs, "the lower passions," and VD. He talked about the prodigal son, and he told a story with an allusion to "the crimson tide of Alabama," the University of Alabama's football team.

"The Christian life is one of renunciation, hardship. . . . He's calling you to a battlefield. . . . It's not easy. . . . It's rough to be a Christian, it's tough to be a Christian."

How "rough" or "tough" did it seem for the white, prosperous Middle America crowd that heard a beloved superstar tell them well-known and acceptable things? His closest reference to ugliness or danger came when he expressed fear that millions might die of starvation in central Africa before Christmas. He lashed out at the fact that Americans feed their pets, at the cost of millions of dollars, while people in other parts of the world starve. Heavy applause greeted this remark. It came from people who would shortly return home to their well-fed pets, and for whom Africa was safely distant from the hearts of American cities.

Billy Graham's interaction with the crowd was practiced and predictable. It was often warm, engaging, even jocular.

Yet Mr. Graham was isolated. This seems to be a factor in his apparent lack of moral fervor. He had written recently, "A taxi driver in one of our largest cities said to me, 'This whole city is corrupt.' " Suddenly I thought to myself that Mr. Graham should ride subways more often, walk the city streets (the hell with taxis and limousines), *get out with ordinary people in their own contexts,* and find out what was really happening to them outside of his own VIP isolation and celebrity status. He seemed out of touch with the realities of contemporary American life, the whole lives of people.

He told the assembled youths to witness for Christ "by the smile on your face." He did not mention Watergate, a moral issue that Amos or Jeremiah—and certainly Jesus—would feel compelled to mention with some urgency. Not as "social action" or an anecdote concerning "the world." But as a parable depicting faithlessness in God, lovelessness toward other children of God, and arrogance that seeks to abrogate the moral code identified with the kingdom of God—*to become as gods.*

In my opinion he did not adequately relate the implications of God's becoming human in Jesus Christ for people who cry out today from the crosses on which they themselves are crucified. Nor on "Youth Night" did he even make passing reference to a religious and moral question so close to the consciences and lives of thousands of youths: amnesty.

He did not mention slums and the absence of equal opportunity in America, or that participating in the liberation of people is actual work of salvation.

"You don't have to rebel. . . . You don't have to go away."

But he addressed himself to his definition of morality.

"I know young men and women who live clean and pure. You don't have to have sex before you're married."

Inasmuch as he spoke during the American summer of 1973, and as perhaps the leading religious figure in America, it seemed incomprehensible to me that Mr. Graham did not take one step further and speak of sexism. But he did not refer to the freedom in Christ that one discovers in sex, in the place of repression and negative puritanical taboos; he did not speak about the new freedom sought by women rebelling against being victims of exploitation as women; he did not speak of the freedom in Christ that is offered by God to the male or female homosexual—in the wholeness of love and with the full dignity of the *imago dei.* Mr. Graham utterly failed to relate the gospel of Jesus Christ to sex when he spuriously discussed sex in the American summer of 1973. Night fell over the Minnesota Fairgrounds and bright lights shone on Billy Graham as he spoke and gestured on the distant podium.

"The government is so big it can't get back to ideals," someone seated next to me said. "So is religion. Graham is trapped in bigness and he can't get out. It's appropriate that his platform is in the center of a racetrack. The two American passions are packaging and speed."

Evangelism, it seems to me, is showing forth the glory of the Lord in the very living of a life. It has little or nothing to do with techniques or even a self-conscious style. It is a life that is moon-drenched, burned through by the sun, a speck of color that one may miss altogether unless one looks quite patiently for its sign, ecstasy amid a lack of expectation, plain truth. It is sacrifice without self-pity, giving oneself without making announcements about it, the gift of healing, unsentimental love that sees beneath masks of success and failure.

We've all known a few evangelists during our lives. Their voices may be quiet as whispers or pealing like bells, but they unmistakably convey an irresistible passion for the love of God and the holiness of life. The evangelists I've known include three schoolteachers, a postman, an elderly friend of mine over many years who died in her mid-nineties, a serious child, a comic child, a score of students, a gardener, and a lawyer. It would not have occurred to them to wear piety in public. They spoke very little about God, who looked out at me through their open eyes.

On the other hand, I have met startlingly few evangelists in the noisy, crowded arena of American organized religion.

At the fairgrounds I sat at the back of the giant crowd looking at Billy Graham. I had read his books, I had seen him on television. I had attended another of his rallies several years earlier in New York City. In Switzerland I had once met him briefly and shaken his hand. What was my strongest impression of him?

Graham's theological isolation from the deep currents of religious thought and the impulses of contemporary Christian action was obvious and saddening. Graham seemed not to know the theology of liberation that has emerged prophetically from the Third World and opened the minds and consciences of countless Christians who had too long seen Jesus Christ as American, white, and middle-class.

"The Kingdom and social injustice are incompatible," Gustavo Gutierrez writes in his seminal book *A Theology of Liberation*. He says: "When justice does not exist, God is not known; he is absent."

Graham seems isolated in class, race, and culture; one finds no evidence that he comprehends the sort of thing that Gutierrez—for example, in his insistence upon naming the political-conflictual dimensions of the gospel as well as its personal-conciliatory aspects—expresses. Gutierrez speaks of conversion: "It means thinking, feeling, and living as Christ—present in exploited and alienated man."

Graham is significant because he represents religion for millions of people; he talks of Christ to them. Yet what Graham says, and represents in a visible life-style, is either irrelevant or literally opposed to what many other Christians believe and practice.

Take an example, again from Gutierrez. He speaks for these Christians when he writes about sin:

> (It) is not considered as an individual, private, or merely interior reality—asserted just enough to necessitate a "spiritual" redemption which does not challenge the order in which we live. Sin is regarded as a social, historical fact, the absence of brotherhood and love in relationships among men, the breach of friendship with God and with other men, and, therefore, an interior, personal fracture. When it is considered in this way, the collective dimensions of sin are rediscovered.*

* From *A Theology of Liberation* by Gustavo Gutierrez. Maryknoll, N.Y.: Orbis Books, 1973, p. 175.

Graham seems to regard sin as primarily personal and sexual and does not bother to relate to sin what Gutierrez calls sinful. So Graham doesn't say much about institutional violence, what it does to people in the name of the state or big business or the military or even in the name of God, *as sin*.

Yet if Christian is to survive as Christian and not a travesty that masquerades under that name, a whole new kind of Christian life must be defined and evidenced. This new kind of Christian life must seek to know the bases of society that are sinful and expend its major effort to change these.

One such change needs to increase social ownership of the means of production, especially in the Third World, where ownership of means of production has often tended to be absentee and American. The American church, fattened with institutional wealth and privilege, scarcely understands what this means—certainly not from the standpoint of socioeconomic victims of big government and big business.

This is not in any sense to say that the individual can be forgotten in the context of Christian. Each of us is created in the image of God. Christ died for each of us on the cross. His Resurrection from the dead is shared with us. The Holy Spirit, alive and active in the world, communicates with us.

The personal search for meaning and fulfillment, whether in myself or others, is something for which I hold the utmost respect. There will always be the personal search, the private crying out to God. But the answer to the cry and the end of the search are linked to the commonalty that comprises other people. One needs to see the relation of one's problem (perhaps it is hunger, or sex, or loneliness) to the needs of others. To find an answer or a solution for oneself is, at the deepest levels of life, to share in solidarity with others whose needs are also met.

Our individual deeds are linked to all the world. There are actions that intrinsically harm others. Perhaps we didn't intend such harm at all. We merely disturbed someone else's peace. We merely consumed more than our share of energy or food, and so someone else must perish.

As he stood in the Minnesota State Fairgrounds, Billy Graham appeared to be almost a Mount Rushmore figure when he addressed the partisan but passionless crowd that had been carved out of Middle America.

"I lived in the South, where we had segregation," he said. "Some of the best friends that I had were black. They went to one church or school, and we to another . . . It wasn't long after I received Christ that something inside me said that something was wrong about that."

At this moment I felt that he was the latest in a succession of spokesmen for the practice of religion that is referred to by James P. Comer, M.D., in his book *Beyond Black and White*. Dr. Comer wrote:

> Africans kidnapped for transport to North America entered a vast, rich, undeveloped country. Because of the limitless frontier, neither government nor religion exercised any real deterrence upon the abuse and exploitation of people who could not protect themselves. Yet the rhetoric of religion and enlightenment was everywhere. The rhetoric of a rigid and restricting religion forced wrongdoers to deny wrongdoing. The rhetoric of a revolution for a noble cause increased the need to deny social evils. This boded ill for blacks.

Most blacks did not expect a "theology of liberation" from Mr. Graham. A black woman social worker in Minneapolis told me, "He runs his mouth and is so out of touch that he probably doesn't realize what he is saying." She was referring to Mr. Graham's comment in South

Africa that he believed rapists should be castrated ("I think when a person is found guilty of rape he should be castrated —that would stop him pretty quick"), as well as his later comment that he "regretted" making it. ("My comment on rape was an offhand, hasty, spontaneous remark at a news conference that I regretted almost as soon as I said it.")

Ours is the age of publicity. Inevitably, Christian efforts to evangelize—to tell the story of Jesus Christ in a compelling way that will communicate sin, repentence, and salvation—become intertwined with the mass media.

I remember when a church official admonished Christian communicators that not to make use of TV and radio would be as unthinkable as if St. Paul had refused to travel in ships or Luther and Calvin had considered the printing press unworthy of use. However, a dilemma injects itself into this discussion when one realizes that the media bear their own values.

When witnessing for Christ becomes itself a form of exploitation, values have clearly plunged into a topsy-turvy fall that is utterly discombobulating. The person witnessing for Christ has forgotten that the gospel is not a product; it stands in judgment upon the methods utilized to communicate it. Of course, it's always worst when religion and politics combine their power and ambition to exploit, dominate or—God forbid—enslave people.

I thought of this when Mr. Graham called for people who were present at the Minnesota State Fairgrounds on July 16, 1973, to "come forward" to make a decision for Christ.

"I want Jesus Christ to have all of me . . . (*Music swells*) . . . You may be Protestant, Catholic, or Jewish . . ."

Later the thousands poured out of the fairgrounds toward their cars, on their way home to watch TV.

"Graham is one of the things that happens when you are success-motivated, as we're trained to be in America," a woman in the crowd said. "It's not substance or quality that counts. It's how many people were there, how many letters were mailed out, how many phone calls were made. That's success. It's a vacuum."

But few people in that vast crowd seemed to share her criticism.

Back in 1955, Mr. Graham told the *Observer* of London: "I am selling the greatest product in the world: why shouldn't it be promoted as well as soap?" Mr. Graham has long and faithfully sold the gospel as a product, using devices that worked for secular success.

Perhaps this is precisely why Mr. Graham so desperately failed to communicate any real sense of personal transformation in Christ. His showmanlike, matter-of-fact, learned-by-heart message seemed not to comprehend at all the dark midnight of the soul. His was a sunny litany, bright and crisp. It was about Christ—but where was Christ in it?

Some supporters of Mr. Graham have criticized Christians who preach an allegedly "social gospel." Surely it is inadequate to espouse social activism without the inner spiritual content of conversion and transformation in Christ, on the one hand, as it is to speak of personal salvation without a radically sacrificial concern for the needs of others and the transformation of society in the image of God, on the other.

This takes on fresh meaning in a world such as ours that is apparently fast approaching one of the great turning points in human history. The meaning of Christian as individual has to take on a deeper dimension of sacrifice and union with other lives.

I find a heartbreaking and triumphant illustration of this in the life of Néstor Paz, a Bolivian Christian youth whose commitment to Christ meant the sacrifice of his life. This commitment found concrete expression in a guerrilla action for the cause of freedom and against one of the most repressive governments in Latin America.

Young Paz died of starvation on October 8, 1970, the day before his twenty-fifth birthday. His was an act of free will for the sake of his Lord and people in desperate need. He kept a journal which has been published under the title *My Life For My Friends.* Generally the notes in his journal were addressed to his young wife. But on Saturday, September 12, 1970, his salutation was different.

> My dear Lord: It's been a long time since I've written. Today I really feel the need of you and your presence. Maybe it's because of the nearness of death or the relative failure of our struggle. You know I've always tried to be faithful to you in every way, consistent with the fulness of my being. That's why I'm here. I understand love as an urgent demand to solve the problem of the other—where you are.

Later in this entry he wrote:

> Ciao, Lord, perhaps until we meet in your heaven, that new land that we yearn for so much.

Watching Mr. Graham at his big rally, I knew I preferred a simpler and purer form of evangelism, the life-style of individual Christians sharing ideals and work in solidarity with other people. A bread-and-butter issue for me was that I did not want church and state to draw close together in a tragic misuse of religion. I feared and disliked manipulating great crowds, charisma that inevitably exploits people, and klieg lights in the night.

I want to be saved from a superchrist in a superstate.

III

Images and Incense:
Popular Religion
and Christian

The first time my name was announced and I walked out from the back of the darkened, crowded room onto the small stage, I was badly frightened. It reminded me of how I had felt, in 1961, boarding a freedom-ride bus in the deep south. My mouth was dry, my heart pounding, I didn't know what in the world was going to happen, and I was committed to a course of action.

I was inside a San Francisco nightclub called the hungry i. As a matter of fact, I wasn't just inside the bloody club, but I was—I guess there's no other word for it—entertaining there. Some patrons might argue about the fact that what they got was entertainment, but I was surely being paid for trying, and contributing my salary to the civil rights movement. Inside the hungry i I read some of my contemporary prayers and just talked with people.

Perhaps the best known of my prayers was "It's morning, Jesus," from my book *Are You Running With Me, Jesus?* that had just recently been published. I opened my reading with it:

It's morning, Jesus. It's morning, and here's that light and sound all over again.

I've got to move fast . . . get into the bathroom, wash up, grab a bite to eat, and run some more.

I just don't feel like it, Lord. What I really want to do is get back into bed, pull up the covers, and sleep. All I seem to want today is the big sleep, and here I've got to run all over again.

Where am I running? You know these things I can't understand. It's not that I need to have you tell me. What counts most is just that somebody knows, and it's you. That helps a lot.

So I'll follow along, okay? But lead, Lord. Now I've got to run. Are you running with me, Jesus?

This was my big fling with "evangelism." I put it in quotes because I'm not sure if it really was evangelism. I have a feeling that evangelism is essentially the way one lives and interacts with people and the rest of life, and precisely what one does at a gut level about furthering love and justice in the world. Somehow I doubt that it is getting up to read prayers in nightclubs, or preaching about Jesus Christ in East Rooms of White Houses and vast arenas, or buying prime TV time to have one's religious say.

Anyhow. I wasn't frightened at the hungry i after that first night in September, 1966. Yet this isn't to say I ever had merely an easy or comfortable feeling. Each night—in fact, each of the two shows every night Monday through Thursday, and the three on Friday and Saturday—held its own mysteries. There could be a hard pocket of hostility within an audience, or just warmth; feelings within people could find open expression, or, far worse for me, remain bottled up inside them. But it couldn't be this simple because the bottled-up feelings would stand there like great unyielding stones, and I couldn't get through at all.

I had moments of severe pain and sadness while on the hungry i's stage. And moments of great joy and fulfillment.

All of these were in relation to other people. One man stayed through a whole show just making nasty remarks and forbidding an open relationship or dialogue between us; this was terribly difficult. Another man, slightly more drunk than the first, fired questions at me and unburdened himself of frankly derogatory remarks. But with him I had an entirely different feeling; he was trying, in his own way and under awkward circumstances, to get into relationship and dialogue with me. I felt we made it.

I'd get tired. Being on stage until 2 or sometimes 3 A.M. is, I found, quite an exhausting experience. Yet the late shows could be the best. One Sunday morning at around 3 A.M., when I was still on the stage, I suddenly realized how, for most of the people in that particular audience, this was church. It was so quiet you could really have heard a pin drop in the room. A few players, actresses and actors from various San Francisco shows, had come in, put their feet up on the stage and placed their drinks there, too, and a kind of community developed naturally.

A favorite, and very personal, prayer from *Are You Running With Me, Jesus?* seemed best to fit this mood and the occasion:

> I've searched for community in many places, Jesus.
> I was often looking in the wrong places, but I don't think my motive was altogether wrong. I was looking futilely and hopelessly there for fellowship, belonging, and acceptance.
> Now, in this moment, which many people would label "loneliness," or "nothingness," I want to thank you, Jesus. In this moment—in this place and with these other persons—I have found community where and as it is. It seems to me it is your gift.
> I am here with these others for only a few hours. I will be gone tomorrow. But I won't be searching so

desperately any more. I know I must accept community where you offer it to me. I accept it in this moment. Thank you, Jesus.

Each show had to represent, I felt, a whole new breakthrough from religion to life. Each audience was new, so it had its own hangups about a priest sitting on a bar stool and talking in a nightclub, a clerical collar up there under the amber light, frank talk in the name of God about sex and race, and finding new reality instead of escapism inside a San Francisco pleasure district.

I would get waves of reaction from people, whether in strong silence or loud applause, sudden laughter or a hushed reaction to something I had just said.

It's hard for me to remember hard specifics concerning what happened at the hungry i. But let's look at press reports. The *New York Times* reported one question that I was asked and my response to it. " 'Are you bringing Jesus into the hungry i?' a patron in the basement establishment of Enrico Banducci asked the cleric. 'How can I?' he replied. 'He's already in the hungry i.' " This query was posed during a question-and-answer period after more than an hour of my reading homilies and original prayers, the latter spoken to a guitarist's accompaniment.

The *Times* continued: "One much appreciated prayer beginning, 'They say he's rocking the boat, Lord,' was about a professor. 'I think he's at Berkeley, unless he's been canned,' Father Boyd said. 'But your Mr. Reagan hasn't gotten there yet and I hope to God he doesn't,' he added amid a burst of applause. This was a reference to the announced intention of Ronald Reagan, the Republican nominee for Governor, to appoint, if elected, a blue-ribbon commission to investigate the University of California at Berkeley."

More details about the event were reported in the *Los*

Angeles Times, which said: "One heckler left toward the end of the performance, shouting 'Boo!' as he went. A woman's voice rose from somewhere in the crowded room. 'Oh, hush up!' and the audience seemed with the priest."

The *Los Angeles Times* continued: "When someone demanded toward the close of his performance, 'Are you God?' he replied: 'Oh, hell no, man. I just try to understand what it means to be a human in this world and what a man's relationship to God is.' He scorned those who 'frown on profanity, a little bit of profanity, and won't let a black or a Jew move into their neighborhood,' and he got applause for saying it. At the conclusion of his performance, the priest was applauded so long that he read another prayer as an encore."

The paper quoted me as saying: "If I had cut some of the pain and the Cross, it might have been a slicker nightclub act, but I think the Cross belongs there. The Gospel was in there, with its redemptive quality. It has to be controversial, because it is the Gospel."

When I was most tired and discouraged, I would remind myself why I was in the hungry i. Not to be on the make for a career, money or publicity, but to serve Jesus by trying to serve people. This would always cool me, restore patience if not energy, and at least provide a focus for the whole thing.

When my material seemed so obviously rough or unstructured, I would remind myself that, if my "act" became polished and expertly professional, I'd need to drop it. For authentic Christianity represents a scandal and an offense, and this must be reflected somehow always in form as well as content. Yet I tried to be professional about timing, use of the microphone, response to the audience, and keeping my own fatigue under control. I believed that I had become a worker-priest, with definite work responsibilities as a part of my obedience to God.

My awareness of a rapidly expanding biblical and

theological illiteracy, coupled with the church's defensive posture of withdrawing further and further from the sights and smells of real life, led me to evaluate different tasks in Christian communication and to undertake a few myself. One of the latter was my appearance at the hungry i.

A bread-and-butter issue for me is the question: How can the Christian faith be communicated? Indeed, is it often communicated inadvertently and outside the pale of self-conscious efforts to do so? And, by the same token, does it frequently elude all sorts of ambitious and even well-meaning attempts to communicate it?

Society itself is in flux. Rules have presently become blurred: sexual, political, ethical. Language as we know it —the exhumed Watergate tapes afford the best evidence of this—has fallen into disuse. Attention span is brief. Idols and ideas alike are given a short run in the celebrity arena. "Instant" is the mercurial arbiter. Confusion and change exist where once there was at least a religious center of reference and awe, if not belief. Familiar words, phrases, and images had their place in a commonly accepted lexicon and folklore. This is no longer the case.

Against the background of such inescapable realities of life, my appearance at the hungry i took place. Its chief point of interest for me now is found in the reactions of various people to the event as an example of Christian communication. Such reactions were best expressed in letters that I received at the hungry i.

Two ministers were affirmative in their reactions. One wrote:

> What a fantastic opportunity to reach so many people who would never go near a church at the "holy hour" Sunday morning. I'm sure most of the parishioners of this bastion of the San Francisco "establishment" think a priest in a nightclub is shocking. I think it's great,

and I hope you do it often. "Varieties of gifts but the same Spirit," as the saying goes.

The other clergyman wrote:

My wife and I were in your "congregation" Monday night. It was the most effective and, for my money, gutty evangelism I've observed in a long time. Some young couple going out next to us commented: First, she said—"He seemed a little nervous, didn't you think?" And he responded—"Hell, you'd be nervous too, reading prayers to a group like us." Nervous or not, you came across.

At the close of my prayer-reading and rapping with the people, I asked for questions. A student at Stanford University commented about this in a letter that he wrote to me.

One friend of mine said to another in a religious argument, "You've got all the answers, but none of the questions." I didn't quite grasp what he had said at the time but after hearing you it means a lot. That's what you did at the 'i.' You put forth the questions, offering no 'pat' or intellectualized answers which so often save people from the chore of thinking.

I was in a state of intense excitement after I left the hungry i. You've probably felt that way; thoughts whirling through your brain at a mile a minute. When I got home I sat down at this table and wrote to myself, almost till dawn. The last thing I wrote was "I better get off my ass and do something—if you think positive, act positive—activate yourself."

I am just being born. At 24, it's not too late. I've lived the first part of my life for myself. I hope to devote the rest to helping others. This is not purely selfless. I suspect it will be more rewarding than living for the big ME could ever be.

On the stationery of a San Francisco hotel, someone wrote the following letter, presumably having put pen to paper following one of the hungry i performances.

The lights come on. Bright. A man stood there. A priest! After the manner of Melchisedek?

He spoke. Of man's inhumanity to man. The church. Life. Injustice. The march. His compulsion to march. Black. White.

"I am told I am white. What is white?"

Who was he asking? You know no color.

Only the heart. You know pure. You know impure. You do not know white. You do not know black.

Jesus.

The church was a building he said. He said the church is really people. Selah.

His language. Coarse. Offensive. Shocking.

At times. A woman arose—protesting—to leave.

Music, Lighting effects, photographer, dark.

Light, strange prayers, music, dark.

Light, strange prayers, music, dark. Photographer.

Sensationalism? Sham? Irreverence? Blasphemy?

Only you know

Jesus.

He's not an ex-father. In. Stay in.

Not out. In.

In. In. In, Father Boyd. Stay in.

He heard you. Is he in?

Jesus.

I had as many questions about what I was doing at the

hungry i as anybody else did. For I was concerned about the precise moment when evangelism turns into exploitation. The latter is inevitably sugarcoated, manipulative of human emotions and feelings, and geared to success on the basis of telling people what they want to hear. Needless to say, I tried to eschew this.

One of meditations seemed so abrasive that some people begged me to delete it because they said that "it turned people off."

What was Hiroshima like, Jesus, when the bomb fell?

What went through the minds of mothers, what happened to the lives of children, what stabbed at the hearts of men when they were caught up in a sea of flames?

What was Auschwitz like, Jesus, when the crematoriums belched the stinking smoke from the burned bodies of people? When families were separated, the weak perished, the strong faced inhuman tortures of the spirit and the body. What was the concentration camp like, Jesus?

Tell us, Lord, that we, the living, are capable of the same cruelty, the same horror, if we turn our back on you, our brother, and our other brothers. Save us from ourselves; spare us the evils of our hearts' good intentions, unbridled and mad. Turn us from our perversions of love, especially when these are perpetrated in your name. Speak to us about war, and about peace, and about the possibilities for both in our very human hearts.

I hammered insistently at themes of personal honesty and social justice. Yet the very glamour and publicity that went hand in hand with appearing at the hungry i provided hard ambiguities.

Evangelism is different from exploitation. H.A. Hodges noted in *Christianity and the Modern World View*:

> People must be told, for it is a central point of Christianity, that their present values are wrong, not merely those which they themselves recognize to be self-centered, but even those of which they are really proud, and that neither in this world nor in Christianity can these be realized at all.
>
> Christianity does not exist to satisfy them as they stand, but to correct them; abolishing some, reforming the conception of others, and bringing to life new desires and insights of duty which were not there before. We can say that the Christian life which results from this is a life preferable in quality to any other that man can live, a life of knowledge and freedom; but it is a new life and in some ways a strange one, too.

The same intense concern about the emergence of a new biblically and theologically illiterate generation that led me to the stage of the hungry i also led me to study closely the mechanics of mass culture when these impinged on religion or Christianity. This became yet another task for me in Christian communication. Because I came to believe that if the church refused to get out of its mothballs and communicate in a living way with living people, it would become a ghetto.

But there is also another side to Christian communication. Ours is a continuing learning experience from the fast-moving images afforded us by TV, cinema, and publicity. Rightly or wrongly, for better or worse, we learn fashion, politics, pragmatism, sex, calories—and Christian.

Years ago Brother George Every, writing in a little-known but significant book entitled *Christian Discrimination*, told Christians that they had better develop useful criteria in order to comprehend the nature of words and images, Christian and otherwise, coming into their lives by means of publicity and modern media. His advice was, of course, not heeded. Yet all of us have been taught at the deepest levels of our lives by images seen on stages and screens and in the glasshoused world of publicity.

I sat eighth row center as a guest priestly critic for the *New York Times* at the Broadway opening of a new rock drama in October, 1971. Can Jesus survive *Jesus Christ Superstar*? was the question that I asked myself.

Jesus had recently become the newest pop phenomenon. He was on the stage in both *Jesus Christ Superstar* and *Godspell*. A sporadic religious movement used his name in association with self-styled "freaks." A bumper sticker on a handful of cars even announced: "Honk if you love Jesus." I could not help but wonder if Jesus as a woman (a capital idea) might be offered to us next. If so, would the model be Betty Ford or Shirley Chisholm, Shirley Temple Black or Bella Abzug?

It could only be presumed that cultural interchange with China would reveal a strapping yellow Jesus. Perhaps a Henry Kissinger would bring a young Chinese actor from Peking to Hollywood in order to help set up a new biblical spectacular with the surprise element of a wholly new image for the treadworn ones of the past.

Can Jesus ever simply be himself? It is apparent that many people want to create Jesus in their own image. Activists want an activist Jesus. Several years ago, Pier Paolo Pasolini added pepper to the scriptural stew by giving us an angry cinematic Christ, played with a mystic electric quality and restless vigor by Enrique Irazoqui in the movie *The Gospel According to Saint Matthew*. He overturned the money changers' tables in the temple with a zeal close to fury, becoming a great overnight favorite cult figure with social activists. This was the best religious picture in years.

John the Baptist was not a bearded Charlton Heston in furs, but a man of the people, sweaty and crude. The disciples had wonderfully unhandsome faces, lined by anxiety and suffering but young in new commitment. One saw Jesus with his disciples as a band of poor men, despised by power structures and marked off from respectable dry rot and hypocritical niceties in the face of human need and pain. Pasolini caught on film the offense and scandal of Jesus.

Contemplatives want a pious figure of Christ locked inside the confines of the Twenty-third Psalm. Whites have always demanded a snow-white Lord, preferably with blond hair and blue eyes. Asserting that "black is beautiful," blacks began to pay public attention to a jet Jesus.

Of course, we have grown accustomed to Jesus' face in a spate of Hollywood biblical films. Yet Jesus as a superstar seemed a devastating irony. Most superstars are not executed as common criminals after being flogged half to death. However, Cecil B. DeMille indulged in a Garbo-esque sign of Christly superstardom when he made *King of Kings* in 1927 and ordered H.B. Warner, who portrayed Jesus, to wear a veil on his way to and from the dressing room and to eat his meals alone.

R. Henderson Bland played Jesus in *From the Manger to the Cross*, a 1912 movie. He later noted in a memoir how crowds gave him a superstar treatment precisely because of the part he played. "The crowds around my carriage were so dense that police were told to keep the people back," Bland wrote. "When I left the carriage to take my position in the scene a way was made for me with no word said. Women stepped forward and kissed my robe."

Stage and screen portrayals of Jesus raise a storm of protest and questions from church spokesmen. Is the mystery of Jesus compromised by literal depiction that adheres to such a detail as accurate historical costuming while it falsifies truth in the very presumption of revealing it before one's eyes?

Yet it is absolutely proper for Jesus to be portrayed on the stage and screen. Christian theology teaches that Jesus does not dwell in holy ghettos separated from the joy and misery, the sordidness and beauty, of human life. Jesus, we are told, lived as a human being for thirty-three years on solid earth and continues to dwell as brother and Lord at the central and intimate places of people's lives, where he shares profound involvement in human politics, work, leisure, sexuality, life, and death.

Instead of merely criticizing the portrayals of Jesus on the stage and screen, it behooves churches to ask what images of Jesus they have been communicating to the public—and to what extent they have happily succeeded or deeply failed in that task. I am inclined to see considerable failure. Partially it was erroneous images of Jesus conveyed to me as a child in a plethora of Sunday school classes that led to my being a cynical and sometimes angry atheist in college.

Still another in a long procession of Jesus images awaited me as I sat inside that darkened Broadway theater in the fall of 1971 to watch the premiere of *Jesus Christ Superstar* for the *New York Times*.

The young actor who portrayed Jesus reminded me of Lauren Bacall, especially in the repeated gesture he used to push back his hair. His was a sensual, soft Jesus: often petulant, self-centered, a figure of flaming youth who enjoys flattery and publicity.

Superstar? Is Jesus in the same league with Jacqueline Onassis, the duchess of Windsor, and Averell W. Harriman? Or, say, with Willie Mays, Barbra Streisand, and Ted Williams?

I am more inclined to share the view expressed to me one day by a student at Yale who said: "I don't think much about Jesus. But to say he's a superstar is all wrong. He's the

99

lost face in a crowd. He's the woman in *La Strada*. He's the leper. But he's not a big celebrity standing up over other people."

Many church folk are thankful for any religious or secular crumbs that fall from a fattened table in these lean days. A great big commercial hit that pays attention to Jesus might even make the church seem to be "relevant." (Power to the Apostles.) Youth might be attracted by means of exploitation to unchanged dogma, ritual, and social attitudes. Best of all, Jesus might become news. He might become (say a prayer) a real superstar to fill all the church buildings again. These church folk say, in effect, "Don't criticize this show. Thank God for it."

The god of technical tricks and slick majesty? For this is the god whom director Tom O'Horgan—shades of Cecil B. DeMille's biblical spectaculars—gave us, with enough brashness thrown in to induce praise from the late Mr. DeMille. And also enough theological travesty to boggle the mind. In a myriad of details gone wrong, the Broadway show bore little resemblance to the New Testament. Yet, what is most important, Jesus' mission got misplaced somewhere from drawing board to Star Chamber.

Sometimes *Jesus Christ Superstar* was *Love Story in Jerusalem*. Other times it sadly seemed to be only *The Greening of the Box Office*. But was it a serious work of art? And how did it deal with the Passion of Christ? Since this show was built on the Rock, I decided that one had best look under it.

I asked myself: Is this the Jesus of a significant counter-culture? Not at all. For we see him reject the sick and distressed victims of society who come to him for help. We see a restless and tired "star" Jesus arrogantly send Judas away to the work of betrayal. Fatigue and introspection could have legitimately been portrayed. But despair looms too centrally in Christ, conveying a sense of mission lost and purpose forgotten.

100

In the absence here of depth of feeling, I recollected the profundity and integrity of the multiple crucifixion that is implicitly portrayed in Eugene O'Neill's *Long Day's Journey Into Night*: a calculated reach into the recesses of the soul, a confrontation with quintessential actors who trod the stage of life and wear flesh and bones, as well as lines upon their faces caused by pain.

As in Dali's concept of the Crucifixion, there was clearly the absence of a cross rooted in earth in *Jesus Christ Superstar*. Such lack of specificity leads to those quasi-religious fantasies that obliterate detailed truth. I am not one of those purists who decry the show's bypassing of the Resurrection. After watching Jesus hang on a Daliesque golden triangle (an avant-garde symbol of the cross?) for a glamorous simulation of the Crucifixion, I offered thanks to the pantheon of gods that we were indeed spared a Resurrection. But in its failure to come to terms with the sacrifice of a Christ-figure, or the Passion of Christ, the celebrated Broadway production of *Jesus Christ Superstar* also failed to become a seriously motivated and constructed rock opera.

It was several things: a Rockette operetta, a Barnumian put-on, a religioso-cum-show biz pastiche, and a musical-ized "Sweet Sweetback's Baadasssss Judas Song." The Jews seemed to be guilty, once again, of causing Jesus' death. Jewish priests were seen in ominous, gargoylelike costumes straight out of medieval caricatures. We were thrust against energy without exuberance, torture without tragedy, in this collage-in-motion based upon a celebrated group of musical numbers, several of them splendid and memorable.

Tim Rice and Andrew Lloyd Webber, who wrote *Jesus Christ Superstar*, had something interesting going for them with their best-selling album of songs. The Broadway production changed all that inexplicably. A clean, unambiguous concept became a muddled, religiously controversial show.

The sexuality of Jesus undoubtedly comprised the exhibit A controversy about the show. He and Mary Magdalene fondled and kissed each other; I felt an implicit acceptance of the fact that they had enjoyed intercourse. The exposure of this side of Jesus' humanity understandably drew cheers from the audience, no doubt in reaction against the celibate Jesus of the organized church who has been used traditionally as a major argument against sex outside of (and before) wedlock as well as against homosexuality.

Looking at Jesus as a human being (as well as the Son of God) with sexual feelings is far overdue in our puritanical, sexually hypocritical society. I applaud it. Yet I feel that his sexuality was not handled sensitively or with taste in the inhuman Broadway parody.

I remain critical of other things in the show: a glittering gold shaft descended from "heaven" onto center stage to indicate, I suppose, the presence of God; Jesus looks up when he asks the Father to spare him; the—excuse me—queentessential Herod ruins "King Herod's Song" by making it a campy nightclub number instead of a piece of the mosaic in "the last seven days in the life of Jesus of Nazareth," to quote the program.

The show gave us a confused, tired but plucky Jesus who is going to the cross even if it kills him. Mary Magdalene is a cool, mod, and sincere chick who digs Jesus but senses that he is very different from other men whom she has known. She sings a gentle ditty about the love for him that she feels. However, it is clearly not sufficiently deep a love to bind her to him through his torture and death. My bet is that Mary Magdalene, after a few bad days, a lot of cigarettes, and a gallon or so of black coffee, would be able to submerge memories of Jesus long enough to shack up with next week's superstar in Jerusalem.

Judas's feelings about Jesus provides the real basis for what utterly fictional story line exists between the musical numbers. Judas feels that he is trapped in a terrible role, one scripted by God and directed by Jesus. In this show, four demons assist divinity with the pragmatic dirty work of haunting and wrestling with him. Judas's acceptance of predestination to damnation smacks unappetizingly of Calvinism with bitters. So Judas ended up playing a role instead of himself.

It is an absurd irony that a simplistic success—with a $1 million advance sale—emerged from the ambiguity and violent paradox of Jesus' Passion, presented on Broadway with all dimensions flattened. Even the controversy of Jesus, intellectually ignored in this show, was made marketable in a plastic-ware production that didn't have a soul.

When it was announced that *Jesus Christ Superstar* would be filmed, I only hoped that the movie would not become a star vehicle and that distant locations would not serve as a substitute for the intimacy of human beings engaged in interaction on dusty Palestinian roads, inside simple dwellings and occasional palaces, and at Golgotha. Well, the movie that resulted simply brought to mind my favorite Negro spiritual, as I noted when *Newsday* invited me to review the film.

> Were you there when they crucified my Lord?
> Were you there when they crucified my Lord?
> Oh! Sometimes it causes me to tremble, tremble, tremble,
> Were you there when they crucified my Lord?

The nails were pounded into the old rugged cross with familiar precision. I asked myself: Why do festering illusions leap like full-grown demons from a filmmaker's mind when the time comes to place this hardy perennial story on celluloid?

The film *Jesus Christ Superstar* offers us the same self-indulgent Jesus who screams "Leave me alone!" when the sick and needy crowd about him for help; sadistically and mercilessly—he's not even a decent guy, but a temperamental superstar—sends Judas off to finish his work of betrayal; and stoically offers his Wotan-like Father—before whom he seems to be more Job than Jesus—his life.

Jesus' sacrifice is portrayed here without perception of its mystery, awareness of its context of victory and joy, or even personal resources that would open up his death to others instead of let death simply close in upon himself.

For example, the only words spoken by Jesus from the death-cross in the movie version of *Jesus Christ Superstar* are "Father, forgive them; for they know not what they do" and "My God, my God, why hast thou forsaken me?" We do not hear those words, or perceive those related actions of Christ's, that concerned the thieves with whom he was crucified and his compassionate response to them; the very human interaction concerning Jesus' mother and his beloved disciple, which reflects Jesus' deep concern for others even at the moment of his own torture; or Jesus' own intense humanness as it reached out to the circle of people standing about the cross and was expressed in the words addressed to them: "I thirst."

Jesus is portrayed in the movie as an athlete-for-Christ, blue-eyed, blond, Anglo-Saxon, muscular; and one can almost see him in a men's after-shave lotion commercial made for television. Why—for Christ's sake—didn't they let Jesus be a Jew in *Jesus Christ Superstar?* After all, they took the cast to Israel to shoot the picture there. Doesn't historical location call also for historical accuracy?

Now we come to the heart of the mystery that inexplicably shrouds this movie. It is anti-Semitic. Obberammergau couldn't top this one. Jew-haters, whether in Germany or Arkansas, could rub their hands with glee and chortle loudly—maybe go out and get drunk in a combination of bewilderment and delight that somebody else, no doubt inadvertently, has done their work for them—when they sit down in a theater to see *Jesus Christ Superstar*.

Yet this film was made in Israel with government cooperation, although curiously without its approval. What went wrong? Who is to blame? The problem is a mind-boggler.

The film arrived at a moment in history when there had occured an official relaxation of traditional, Establishment Jewish-Christian relations. After Vatican II had moved resolutely in this direction, a humorous footnote was offered by Harry Golden. He observed that, inasmuch as the Christians had finally absolved the Jews of collective guilt in the death of Christ, maybe the time had come for Jews to convene a world congress to absolve the Christians of collective guilt for the Crusades. A new age had arrived, ecumenically speaking. One could make a joke, and smile.

Then the Six-Day-War, and Christian reactions to it, brought Jews and Christians into an altogether original dialogue that was sometimes painful but broke ground in its candor and creative possibilities. Yet Auschwitz always lurked immediately in the past, eerily and uneasily shadowing the present.

But the movie *Jesus Christ Superstar*, with its G rating which drew in families and youths, equates Jewishness with villainy. Jewish priests, scowling beneath their grotesque hats that resemble medieval caricatures, peer down from a scaffold at the Middle American Jesus who strides up the road surrounded not by sweaty disciples but—of course!—flower children. Theirs is the kingdom; their enemy is organized religion—and this is Judaism, represented before our eyes by unsmiling, conniving, murderous, unprincipled, unloving, always Machiavellian Jewish priests. Voilà!

The film's dialogue introduces Jewish references that

cannot be found in the Bible. Why were they glued onto the script? Pilate addresses the crowd, "Look at me—am I a Jew?" He says, "You Jews produce messiahs by the sackful."

The movie tells the Passion story against a backdrop of modern Israel. So the temple scene shows machine guns for sale—this, a long giraffe's leap from the money changers' tables in the temple. When this is combined with the film's imagery of Judas running from military tanks driven over the desert as warplanes streak through the sky overhead, one has another unmistakable, violent, clear image: Israel as militaristic, a warlike nation possessing invincible power. This lends nothing to the telling of the Christ story. Indeed, it provides the most jarring of distractions.

When the Broadway version of *Jesus Christ Superstar* presented a black Judas, I simply accepted this as a producer's decision. However, black Judas is back again in the movie, and this time I found that I had serious questions about the casting, primarily because of the film's potential impact on a worldwide audience. Let me explain.

There is a scene, for example, where Judas angrily stalks away from Jesus. Dozens of white hands are raised in a praise-and-clapping sequence; superimposed over these is the departing and alienated black figure. This scene will be instantly understood in South Africa or anywhere else— locations are legion—where Manichaeanism still lurks in human minds, that black is night and white is light, black is death and white is Easter lilies of Resurrection.

The producer-director, Norman Jewison (who is not a Jew, despite the fact that many people would ironically construe from his name that he was) has stated that his casting of Judas had to do only with the excellence of the performer.

Yet Black Judas, critically standing apart from Jesus and his followers, speaks in a condemnatory manner of their spending money on ointment when there are "people who are hungry, people who are starving"—this, in an explicit modern Israeli film location. His presence unmistakably suggests a Third World identification. Symbolism in juxtaposition with the film's script speaks for itself.

This racial mark takes on bizarre connotations when Judas says to the Jewish priests, "I don't need your blood money"—an exacerbating line in an era of strained Jewish-black relations in the schools and changing neighborhoods of modern American urban life. Black Judas reaches out for the bag of death money. A Jewish priest drops it on the ground. Black Judas kneels down to pick up the Jewish money, a scowl on his face. Uh-uh. If this was done without any awareness of present racial tension amid urban stress, it reflects an incredible human insensitivity.

Black Judas emerges as a white liberal stereotype of a black man. He and three black female dancers (spin-offs from the Supremes) turn on the rhythm in a movie fantasy way that makes more and more black men and women quite legitimately cringe and say that they are frankly sick and tired of the stereotypes in which they find themselves contained. A white liberal view of black male—as hip, groovy, stud—is ultimately claustrophobic and dehumanizing.

Judas, if he were to be black in this film, could have been a quiet, low-key, thoughtful sort of guy—as so many black men are. Indeed, black caricature is carried so far in the movie that, when Judas commits suicide by hanging himself from a tree limb, the scene calls to one's mind a southern lynching tableau. One cannot help but mentally superimpose on the screen the words *Strange Fruit*.

The most significant aspect of Judas's blackness insofar as *Jesus Christ Superstar* is concerned, however, must be Jesus' white missionary paternalism toward him. Jesus, seen in relation to Judas in this movie, is mockingly his brother's "keeper." Jesus' followers in organized religion have traditionally been sinful racists, while they tried to palm off sin as being sexual.

But for *Jesus Christ Superstar* to suggest personality characteristics in Jesus that delineate feelings of racial superiority, by means of symbol cum non sequitur, raises questions about the film's initial credibility. When Judas asks, in despair, "Why was I chosen?" (for the damning act of Jesus' betrayal), racism looms larger than life. Racists who use biblical fundamentalism as their text for hate traditionally assigned God-given inferiority to the black race.

I have no idea what went awry in the making of this theologically and artistically unsuccessful film. The Herod scene, for example, is so tasteless that a preview audience, seated in a heavy silence where no one seemed to breathe, was left stunned by its fatigued banality.

The ending of the film? Well. A bus prepares to drive off as the various cast members finish climbing aboard. Bravo. Inventive. Refreshing. *Stop there.* But no. We have to go on until a pumpkinlike object (the moon? the sun?) is on the screen. And—you guessed it—standing in front of the object is an empty cross.

Frankly, does it matter in the long run whether a Hollywood screen portrayal of Jesus is good or bad? Does *Jesus Christ Superstar* in Technicolor and Todd-AO 35 make any difference? It does, and I'll tell you why.

Despite its success symbols—real estate, money in the bank, endowments, Establishment connections, and occasional athletic publicity efforts—Christianity does not seem to be on very intimate terms with Jesus Christ.

One is told that the successful preachers in America today offer a practical Christianity directed toward individual needs, because people are more interested in themselves than in society. Such a distorted and partial gospel, in a world that contains Auschwitz, South Africa, and Vietnam, readily explains the troubled crisis of Christianity in western civilization. The habit of churchgoing has not seriously threatened militarism, white racism, institutional persecution of black people and other minorities, and the breakdown in public morality that is partially evidenced by the phenomenon of Watergate.

The tragedy cuts deeper. People call for something in which they can believe. A faith. Computerized nominal Christians—names on a list, bodies in an occasional pew—do not know Jesus Christ as a real person or a personal savior. Take a youth to lunch and find out about the present and the future of contemporary faith.

For western civilization, the implications of this crisis in belief are staggering. Millions of people are not turning away from the person, example, or teachings of Jesus; they are rejecting church-as-usual. They are turning away from a selfish "help me but not my neighbor" parody of serious biblical religion, cynicism encased in the loss of idealism, faith without practice, and the loss of spiritual vitality and dynamism.

Against the backdrop of this existential religious situation, movie Jesuses come and go. Well-meaning but uninformed clergy, anxious to find a secular handle for the communication of the faith as well as a sharp, quick way to draw a big crowd of otherwise alienated youth, respond with alacrity to the promotion propositions of movie press agentry. So these men of the cloth fill buses with Sunday School kids and cart them off to see Jesus in a new "religious" film.

Evangelism! The kids receive an education by way of movie glamour, stars, color, music, and the big screen. These teach them more about God, Jesus, the Holy Spirit, sin, grace, salvation—well, name it—than all the volunteer Sunday school teachers manage to do in their limited time, drab classrooms, and their struggle for secular credibility.

However, the big-time glamour teaching is showbiz entertainment. Cosmetic Christianity, in this or other forms, fails because it lacks content and substance. And what, in the end, went wrong? These kids never asked for a stone; they asked for bread.

This is surely not the fault of movie producers, including Mr. Jewison—whose motives, if not the results of his work, are likely beyond reproach. The problem must be placed at the feet of those church spokesmen who, over the years, have thanked the movie producers for their "relevance," "contributions to the faith," and "religious" pictures.

In 1912, Jesus was portrayed in a film called *From the Manger to the Cross*. Press agents went to work on religious promotion. It was declared inadvisable for theater ushers to be garbed in ecclesiastical vestments. However, exhibitors were advised to burn incense in the theaters shortly before the crowds poured through the doors to see the movie. We need some incense for *Jesus Christ Superstar*.

Godspell offered us yet another theatrical and mass media view of Jesus. I saw the first Los Angeles production of this musical based upon the Gospel according to St. Matthew as a guest priestly critic for the *Los Angeles Times*. A youthful actor played Jesus with a clown's red heart on his forehead and blue paint marks on his cheeks. He appeared first in yellow shorts then changed to striped overalls for the rest of the show.

His followers were clown-like, happy-sad members of what could be a commune of innocent folk. Looking at them, I was reminded of Peter Berger's statement that laughter is the final truth, power the final illusion.

In *Godspell* Jesus teaches his followers in an utterly unsophisticated, light, often humorous manner; his parables are staged in what is made to appear an improvisational style. The show was luminously "conceived and adapted" by John-Michael Tebelak, with music and new lyrics by Stephen Schwartz.

The young Jesus of *Godspell* sparks his followers to act out their own feelings. He does not "star" or dominate the proceedings, and the result is not only refreshing but convincing. A clown? He is a tragedian, too. But his portrayal is singularly unphony because of his refusal to take himself seriously, become morbid, hold a grudge, or pontificate.

"Did I promise an answer to the question?" he quickly shoots back to a follower who has demanded the neatly packaged literalism of an unpoetic answer.

Godspell started slowly for me. I remained skeptical and untouched well into the show. Would this be yet another exploitative Jesus gimmick? Then the gentle tenderness and human quality of the show took hold of me. *Godspell* on stage offered probably the most moving Last Supper I have yet seen, absolutely without posturing or stiff, pious gropings for feeling. The good-byes between Jesus and his followers were bear hugs and warm embraces untouched by devastating despair. Reactions were thoughtful, sensitive and trusting.

An altogether new dimension was given the betrayal scene. Here, it is not Judas's kiss of ignominy that became central. Instead attention was focused upon Jesus' kiss of forgiveness, marked by an absence of fear or personal betrayal. The Crucifixion was a compelling scene suggestive of rock opera.

"Oh, God, I'm dying," said Jesus in *Godspell* as he stood on a simple set where lights simulated the passion of an electric chair death with its jolts and body thrusts.

The youthful Jesus portrayed on the stage in *Godspell* caught the significance of Christian witness. Does a Christian witness in strength or in weakness? Let me put this question another way: Is the strength of Christian witness found in its own weakness and, at the same time, in the strength of Jesus Christ?

Karl Barth once interpreted witness in this moving way:

> A man may be of value to another man, not because he wishes to be important, not because he possesses some inner wealth of soul, not because of something he is, but because of what he is . . . not. His importance may consist in his poverty, in his hopes and fears, in his waiting and hurrying, in the direction of his whole being towards what lies beyond his horizon and beyond his power.
>
> The importance of an apostle is negative rather than positive. In him a void becomes visible. And for this reason he is something to others: he is able to share grace with them, to focus their attention, and to establish them in waiting and in adoration. The Spirit gives grace through him.

Jesus, on the stage in *Godspell*, conveyed this meaning to me. And the portrayal of Jesus' followers somehow caught the meaning of these words written by the American poet Delmore Schwartz in *The Starlight's Intuition Pierced the Twelve*.

> "And I will always stammer, since he spoke,"
> One, who had been most eloquent said, stammering.

However, the movie version of *Godspell* shifted gears. It presented us with something totally unexpected, an arresting symbol of the spirituality of the contemporary era in America's and the world's life. How does one precisely define this? As I wrote in the *Washington Post*, it is bright packaging of spiritual form, benign neglect of abrasive truths concerning human needs, withdrawal from the fervor of social involvement, and the absence of moral passion.

Only half a gospel is told by the film *Godspell*. Its attractive, vivacious, and colorful view of life is not balanced by darker hues, the verities of human savagery, and the depths of loneliness and despair that are to be found, along with belly laughs and gentle dreams, in the city's byways and alleys.

This Jesus, played by Victor Garber, wears a clown's red heart on his forehead, too, along with paint marks on his cheeks, and he performs a nimble song-and-dance routine. Undeniably it is a refreshing change of pace from the plastic Christs of too many Hollywood movies. Yet this Jesus has astonishingly few sharp words to say in protest against the Establishment. He is ultimately pleasant but characterless, and his nickname could be Sunny.

The film casts contemporary spirituality with a Jesus who turns a sad, bland glance at tragedy when he is inescapably confronted by it but would much rather look the other way. Generally he does what he would rather do.

Godspell on the screen relentlessly avoids a familiar Gothic look. It eschews cathedral interiors, crucifixes, pulpits, Sunday schools, incense pots, and anything else that spells church. Instead, it utilizes such disparate, and churchly unfamiliar, elements as explosive human exuberance, mime, and the megalopolitan backdrop of contemporary Manhattan.

This, in my opinion, is fine. Traditional methods of telling the Christ story bogged down long ago in hackneyed techniques of simulated pious expression as well as overly familiar details that became idols and therefore obscured the central message. All of this had to be changed, and *Godspell* changed it. Allegory and poetry are employed here to tell the story in a modern urban context with verve and speed.

The film's representation of the Last Supper is excellent.

113

Theology and art come together gently in the final scene of *Godspell*, directed by David Greene from a screenplay that he wrote with John-Michael Tebelak.

A small, vulnerable band of Jesus' followers, dwarfed in juxtaposition against the buildings of New York City, carries Jesus' body in what can best be described as a funeral-Resurrection procession. Before our eyes the handful of disciples is changed into a teeming crowd of contemporary people roaming Fifth Avenue at noon. The primitive church has moved into the modern world.

Yet a major flaw is that the translation of *Godspell* from stage to screen has lost the intimate audience rapport it had for mime-telling the parables. This basic device of the stage presentation now often becomes coyly heavy-handed, resembling an awful Sunday school class. More important, it is unfortunate that millions of filmgoers, who may well be open to a portrayal of the hope of the Christian gospel as it is rooted in sober realities of the human condition, will see this simplistic view of Christ without being offered a fuller dimension.

One wishes to see the meaning of Christ's life placed in the perspective of human captivity, struggle, and even endemic hopelessness that provided the ambiance of his earthly experience. The gospel certainly addressed the wholeness of life that the film curiously lacks the guts, or imagination, to show.

Franco Zeffirelli's cinematic look at young St. Francis of Assisi, *Brother Sun, Sister Moon*, offered us yet another exhibit piece of warped spirituality. For Zeffirelli's glamorous vision of poverty is an unreal one. He delineates injustice romantically, from a distant and uninvolved vantage point. I am reminded of J. B. Priestley's great definition: "Hell—not fiery and romantic but gray, greasy, dismal—is just around the corner."

It is especially ironic that the film is based on the life of

St. Francis—a rich youth who cast away his possessions, embraced poverty, and inspired a religious order rooted in the idealism of the Beatitudes. The film goes awry. At its conclusion, St. Francis is walking alone toward hills that seem to leap at us from a color page in *Arizona Highways*. I thought that this is a bit like saying have your sacrament and eat it, too. What happened to Francis' involvement with poverty, social injustice, and human pain?

Why did Zeffirelli betray his apparently sincere intention to tell the St. Francis story? The key to this question may be perceived in a remark made in the film to Francis by Pope Innocent III: "In our obsession with original sin we have tended to forget there is also such a thing as original innocence."

Where ought one to look for it? *Lord of the Flies* told us that it cannot be found in youth. Original innocence might best be found inside the Garden of Eden, perhaps alongside a fractured million-dollar vase for the Metropolitan Museum. Outside Eden, however, life is a combination of innocence and ambiguities.

Zeffirelli reveals an obsession for trying to depict beauty without warts, labor minus sweat, and purity without paradox. His portrayal of life in this movie fails precisely where his vision is flawed. His absolute dichotomies between good guys and bad guys—between a "selfless" Francis and his "selfish" father, a "righteous" Francis and a "corrupted" bishop, a "sinless" Francis and a "sinful" pope—lack the truth and reality of shading.

This conjures up the imagery of recent U.S. morality and spirituality, where dissent was apparently equated with treason. For example, one is reminded of Spiro W. Agnew's classic comment concerning "the glib, activist element who would tell us our values are lies" and his proposal "to separate them from our society with no more regret than we should feel over discarding rotten apples from a barrel."

115

One wondered if he later wished to extend his proposal to include the Watergate villains. However, an awareness of life's dimensions and paradoxes inevitably precludes such simplistic formulas, whether these emanate from a speech made by Mr. Agnew or a film made by Mr. Zeffirelli.

The highlight of *Brother Sun, Sister Moon* is a marvelous, but, I should think, unintended combination of high religious camp and human tenderness. Innocent III (played by Alec Guinness in such a diffident way as to make one yearn for Rex Harrison's verve, irony, and energy as Pope Julius II in *The Agony and the Ecstasy*) climbs down from the papal throne in the Vatican, passes by a covey of bejeweled and enraged courtiers, descends a seemingly mile-long mosaic stairway that would do justice to Busby Berkeley, and kisses the bare feet of Francis.

This is a tough act to follow. But as Francis and his followers prepare to depart the papal presence, they are surrounded by pages carrying lighted candles. Now the candles seem gradually to be transformed into tongues of fire, lending the tableau a pentecostal quality that is beguiling. The religious packaging of all this would do justice to a promotional Billy Graham rally and a public relations-engineered national prayer breakfast, the two most conspicuous spiritual monuments of current American history.

Alas, both of these occasions would be more concerned with pie in the sky than food for the hungry, how many bombs fell on Vietnam or Cambodia from U.S. planes, or exactly what it means to be treated-as-nigger. Zeffirelli's lush, expensive, and romantic scene has the same air of decadence and betrayal as a Graham rally or a sanctimonious prayer breakfast, where ugly realities of life—as well as prophetic words and actions about them—are noticeably absent.

Zeffirelli cast his movie with as much care as is required

to cast the White House staff. Graham Faulkner's ivory skin and full red lips suggest a St. Francis by El Greco. Judi Bowker as Clare, a young woman who follows Francis's path of renunciation, seems to have stepped out of a canvas by Botticelli. But both players, resembling costumed marionettes that work under Zeffirelli's taut strings, fail to come to life.

St. Francis, did, in fact, leave us a timeless legacy in his capacity to love. This needs to be translated in such a way as to be eloquent and intelligible for people and situations today. Ours is an era of hollow rhetoric and desperate intentions, gross materialism and false security. Zeffirelli's ultimate failure lies in not finding the sensitive balance between love of God and love of people. St. Francis found it. Franco Zeffirelli does not permit Francis's outreach to us across the centuries into the present era, with its God talk and its sad abuse of people.

Zeffirelli's movie about St. Francis oversells images of an innocence that it does not find. Also, it fails to find truth amid a plethora of beauty—beautiful people in lavish scenes.

So, like *Godspell*, it hauntingly reflects the contemporary world's spirituality. It will be remembered best for religious aridity in the midst of highly publicized religiosity, utterances about morality in the context of grossly immoral behavior, and tranquilized small talk where there was a need for the expression of profound moral outrage combined with vision.

Zorba the Greek, on the other hand, is a profoundly religious film that many people would consider to be sacrilegious.

Nikos Kazantzakis released the vitality and sheer human zeal of Zorba into the one world of art and life. Having long ago become something of a folk hero, it was fitting for Zorba to emerge in film. The event is splendid. For Zorba, despite spurious judgment of more sophisticated men that he is trapped in paradoxes, is, in reality, quite unalienated from the universe, other persons, and his own nature. He keeps affirming life rather than negating it. He sees its tragedy as clearly as any other man, but he experiences its joy more sensitively.

"Life *is* trouble. Only death is not," he says.

Zorba beholds the earth, smells and feels it, and finds it is good. He accepts its blessing.

So the picture poses again the dilemma of how a style of life which seems Christ-derived in its fundamental motivation often is found outside the institutional church, its mores and norms. In addition, we are confronted by a bridge—with its foundations outside the structured church —which brings together the sacred and secular, the holy and profane, because God's world is clearly seen as a unity, not heretically fragmented by such dichotomies.

"I have got to go fast," Zorba says, and the film moves at a breathtaking pace with him yet manages to give us more moments of reflection and changes of pace and mood than other motion pictures in recent memory. Zorba (portrayed by Anthony Quinn) catches life in his mouth like air. Irreverent by pietistic or bourgeois standards, his reverence for life is so strong it is demanding.

What society terms sexual promiscuity is, by Zorba's standard, the giving, as well as the receiving of joy and pleasure. He speaks about God's participation in sexuality in the incarnation itself. Zorba's humanness is not mean; his compassion is unsentimental, knowing, and precise. He has learned well the cynicisms of the world, yet this has wondrously increased his childlike faith in the glory and power of life as something holy to be celebrated, not desecrated by indifference or stoicism as if it were profane.

Zorba adamantly refuses to be bound by accepted order unless he can honor the priority of integrity within that order, and he will not worship security by offering it his life. "A man needs a little bit of madness or else he never dares cut the rope and be free," he tells Basil (Alan Bates), the young Englishman for whom he attempts to operate a mine on the island of Crete.

The mystery and experience of life, for Zorba, can be expressed in a kind of choreography. When Zorba is either very sad or happy, he dances. "If a man is full, what can he do? Burst!" His first dance in the film is dictated by great happiness. The mood quickly shifts. He tells Basil about another time he had danced in intolerable sorrow. "When my little boy died, the dancing stopped the pain."

Basil is a young English writer who has reached a point of numbing introspection and longing; he feels old, momentarily written out, completely unrelated to life and people. Zorba is bothered by Basil's seeming rigidities, lapses of unkindness toward people who strike him as merely amusing or gauche, and the restraint he imperially imposes over passion and compassion within his own life.

"You think too much," Zorba tells his young friend. "With your head you decide, 'this is right, that is wrong.' "

Two women are prominent in *Zorba*. One is Madame Hortense (played by Lila Kedrova), an aged and innocent lady whose small fortune was established on her earnings as an officers' prostitute in a faraway wartime. Her own dance is a gentle reminder of earlier days when she started her search for love, and she offers this, in all the vulnerability of her lost beauty, to Zorba and Basil on the first night they reach Crete.

In a scene of freshness and mercy, Zorba and Madame Hortense are affianced. In a later scene, of fragility and simple trust, she holds Zorba, while reciting a prayer out of her childhood, as she dies. Peasant women, even as she watches from her deathbed, start to ransack and strip clean the room.

The other woman in the film is a young widow (Irene Pappas). Zorba tries to save her life, but her throat is cut by a Cretan father whose son committed suicide after he was told that the widow, whom he loved, had spent the night with Basil. The scene of her death is a barren field marked by its own choreography; she runs desperately from one side to the other while peasants hurl stones at her. Their shouts, and her screams, are partially drowned out by the chanting of priests inside a church where the young suicide is being buried.

And one is reminded again, in art as in life, of the church which does not know or hear human agony; of the church which encases itself in vestments, organization, chanting or ritual, instead of involving itself in the cause of justice at its very doorstep.

Director Michael Cacoyannis has rendered justice, running over, to the Kazantzakis novel. Just before the conclusion of the film, it seems that Zorba and Basil are left with only death and failure. At this moment we see Zorba and Basil, alone together on a bleak stretch of a Cretan shore. Basil, in his own futility and despair, sees that Zorba remains exultant in life. "Teach me to dance," he quietly entreats his friend.

The dance of the two men starts slowly, for Basil must find his way. It builds, as the film itself, to an event of extraordinary integrity, beauty, and vitality. The two men laugh, sharing joy. Renewal has come out of death itself.

An actress friend of the late Noel Coward is reported to have accepted Mr. Coward's invitation to attend a London theater performance, but she said, "If it's a play with a message, I won't dress." Of course, any play Mr. Coward could have taken her to see in London that night—be it a musical, a light comedy or a serious drama—had a message. All plays, all films, have a message. All plays, all films, are theological.

Back in 1850 Christoph Blumhardt, a German pastor, saw the connection between the Bible and the newspaper— between *this* and *that* in Christ. He brought together the men of his church one night each week. One week they would read the Bible together. The next week they would read the newspaper together, interpreting it in the light of God's action in history and in terms of human sin in politics and other spheres of social life.

C.S. Lewis understood this connection when he said, in a lecture delivered in 1942 about *Hamlet* that:

> Its true hero is man . . .haunted man . . . man with his mind on the frontier of two worlds, man unable either quite to reject or quite to admit the supernatural, man struggling, yet incapable of achievement because of his inability to understand either himself or his fellows or the real quality of the universe which has produced him.

I have been highly critical concerning some explicitly religious films. Let me be just as commendatory about another such film, and try to explain why. *Essene* is one of the best religious films ever made. This, despite the fact that it lacks a temple rape, a chariot race, a trace of brimstone, or even a sound track of God shouting through echo chambers. It is talky, intellectual, and has no stars.

But brace yourself for the intensity in *Essene* and fasten your safety belt. Before the film has ended, a viewer has been plummeted into an ecclesiastical *Who's Afraid of Virginia Woolf?* with emotions rawly exposed.

Fred Wiseman's cinema verité look at life inside a monastery also studies the essential meanings inherent in any institutional framework and ponders how history and/or eternity impinges upon present time. It is the sixth in a series of Wiseman's films on vital American institutions (others have included *Law and Order, Hospital,* and *Basic Training*).

Essene (the title comes from the name of an ascetic brotherhood founded in the second century B.C.) is about the round of ordinary daily life inside an Anglican monastery in rural Michigan. The time is the summer of 1971. The monks engage in farming in order to earn a living. Their religious community is small. The reason for the community's existence is to worship and glorify God.

Yet the revolution that is apparently taking place in most contemporary institutions has certainly also touched the life of organized religion. So the film depicts how some younger monks feel strongly that there need to be additional reasons for the community to exist. One of these is to enrich and deepen the human interrelationships within communal life itself. Another can be described as relating more directly to the flow of expression and ideas in the world outside of the monastery.

It is apparent from the film that considerable tension exists within the community concerning how to bridge the gap between its ingrown existence on the one hand and the problems and rigors of modern urban society on the other. In the midst of a quiet chapel service, a hooded young monk passionately interjects an intercession for the victims of Hiroshima. Another monk speaks to his brethren intensely and at length about a therapist in New York City who once helped him and asks the community's prayers for her.

Only a single scene in *Essene* takes us outside the monastery itself. It is a warm vignette that has a picaresque touch. An older monk, who is identified in the film as a cantankerous and often obstructive member of the community, goes shopping in a nearby town for such needed items as a potato peeler and a toilet seat.

Back in the monastery we saw him argue vehemently against anyone there calling him by his first name, saying that he preferred the formal title of "brother." However, now inside the town store, a clerk repeatedly addresses him by his first name, while the monk smiles happily, obviously enjoying the experience.

This raises a question: Would he be better off if he could spend considerably more time away from the confines of the monastery and in contact with a broad cross section of people? Or could the community vigorously open itself to an influx of different people as well as ideas and more varied aspects of life? Yet this would necessitate radical changes in the community's assessment of its nature and functions.

The film mostly shows us the monks engaged in worship, group sessions that are at least implicitly involved in amateur therapy, and work. We see little recreation, small talk, wasted time, or solitariness. The community is white, with the exception of one monk who appears to be oriental and another who might be black. *Essene's* central figure is the middle-aged, sturdy, and reflective abbot. He reveals a capacity for listening patiently to other people speak their minds. The abbot seems to limit his authority from time to time but never lets go of it.

A young monk is given a central role in Wiseman's film. At first we see him crying as he says to a nun that he has been lacerated by the monastic experience and is anguished. Later, in a group session, he speaks of "conflict, anger, and bitterness," of feeling "unhappy, lost, wounded, crippled," and asks his brethren, "Will you pray for me?" They crowd around him, singing and praying, kissing and holding him and placing their hands upon his head and body.

I suppose that I have not experienced a more powerful moment in film than one in *Essene* when that monk, seated at a piano, plays and sings "Deep River." His song moves in ups and downs, highs and lows, loudly—now he is bellowing and shouting—and then softly.

It expresses yearning and longing, without the slightest

repression, for fulfillment and wholeness. The scene is somehow heartbreaking and triumphant at one and the same time.

"I want to cross over . . . cross over . . . cross over," he prays.

How can a film express a religious experience? By showing a human being having one.

Watching the monks seated in their refectory eating a meal in silence, I was reminded of Walter M. Miller, Jr.'s book *A Canticle for Leibowitz*, with its vision of a monastery located in some future embattled age, attempting to maintain a semblance of order and preserve humanistic as well as religious values.

The grasp of a similar vision could explain why Wiseman selected the monastery, with its ancient and medieval connotations, as a symbolic modern institution for filming. However, one cannot but wonder with what mixed emotions and motives the monastic order decided (by a community majority vote? by the abbot's decision?) to lend itself to the tricky, vulnerable, and ambiguous experience of exposing itself to the mass media on film.

One discovers a universal denominator in *Essene* when the novice master vents feelings of frustration about his job and asks for more community support in meeting his day-to-day problems of working with new recruits to the order. At this moment he could be the dean of a college, a precinct leader, an army sergeant, a hospital administrator, or a harassed editor.

Inversely, a uniqueness about the institution of the monastery is illustrated when the novice master blurts out to the abbot: "You have been saying this for eighteen years and you're still asking for specifics." Eighteen years!

Unlike the hip urgency of a high-powered business conference, discussion in the monastery meanders like a slow-moving stream. Decision-making itself is the least important part of it. Instead, the growing relations between people and their very character development inevitably take precedence.

The high mobility in hospitals, political alliances, ad agencies, colleges, newspapers and the military—ought one to include the family?—would not permit that casual remark to be made in most other American institutions.

Essene has no real beginning or ending. It is a fluid, extraordinarily honest and nontheatrical experience that stands in stark contrast to extravagant, banal, celebrity-studded revivalist hours purchased in prime-time TV or the million-dollar treacly spiritual thuds coming out of a Hollywood factory.

Fred Wiseman conveys humility without resorting to humble expressions, an awareness of profound piety without mock spirituality. Wiseman's relentless camera's eye probes exasperating stubbornness or an attentive glance, inspects openness of spirit or hands tightly clasped. Silences are practiced and respected.

An ordinary viewer whose life is not directly touched by religion will meet in *Essene* religious people who have a passion for sharing their loneliness. They are obsessed by questions of belief and meaning. This immediately sets them apart from an average viewer who is face to face with the pragmatic exigencies of daily survival and competition.

While the people in *Essene* live in slow motion, an average viewer runs to the rhythms of the clock-auto-jet age. *Essene*, then, must be a vastly out of the ordinary experience for a viewer. How will he/she relate to it? The anti-show biz ambiance that pervades the film from start to finish may curiously be a factor in winning it a large selective audience. For a viewer may find the unvarnished verities in *Essene*, along with the rough candor of their presentation, downright refreshing.

And let's face it: the question of God, quite aside from religious trappings or theological density, remains one of the two or three big questions that actually absorb people. *Essene* raises the question of God urgently and eloquently.

A viewer will observe the monks as they ritualistically exchange the liturgical "kiss of peace" in the mass but live according to precepts that include celibacy in the place of customary sexuality, and as they engage in hard work without earning money for themselves. So a viewer will frankly be confronted by yet another question: Are these monks wise men or idiots, socially useful or detrimental, irrelevant dropouts from the mainstream of contemporary life or perhaps modern saints? Fred Wiseman presents a point of view but does not provide an answer. The viewer must do that.

We have seen how mass media imagery can distort—as it can also on occasion reinforce—images of Christian in an age of technology, publicity, and communications power. It is ironic that media portrayals of the seamy, disillusioned, and even despairing side of life often provide a clearer glimpse of Christian authenticity than simply routine and dimensionless portrayals of religious subjects.

The former can sometimes let us look straight into a human mind or soul for a shattering and illuminating moment of truth and see a life that longs for peace, redemption, joy, love, wholeness.

"None of us can help the things that life has done to us," the mother cries out in Eugene O'Neill's drama *Long Day's Journey Into Night*. "They're done before you realize it, and once they're done they make you do other things until at last everything comes between you and what you'd like to be, and you've lost your true self forever."

This is *praeparatio evangelica*, preparation for the Christian gospel's proclamation that one's sins are forgiven in the very act of honest and humble repentance, and one is restored by Christ.

Nothing in the literature or the mass media of my lifetime

has moved me more deeply than the agony and the dilemma of a woman in Rose Macaulay's comic and deadly serious novel *The Towers of Trebizond*.

The woman's lover, a man who was married to someone else during the time they had a long affair, has died in an automobile accident that was the woman's direct responsibility. Because of their illicit relationship, the woman had long felt unworthy to receive the church's sacraments, and now she perceives that a return to the church would even be a gesture against the past that she fully shared with her lover.

> Someone once said that hell would be, and now is, living without God and with evil, and being unable to get used to it. Having to do without God, without love, in utter loneliness and fear, knowing that God is leaving us alone for ever; we have driven ourselves out, we have lost God and gained hell. I live now in two hells, for I have lost God and live also without love, or without the love I want, and I cannot get used to that either. Though people say that in the end one does. To the other, perhaps never.

I have thought and felt the same way. Yet now I strongly disagree with two of the woman's assumptions. I wish that she were here and I could argue with her about them. First, I do not believe that she does live "without God and with evil." The breaking of a church law is not to be equated with living "with evil." I find the woman in the book to be a loving, amusing, generous, courageous person; I find—despite her protestations to the contrary—that she lives with God.

Secondly, I do not believe that we have any way of knowing that "God is leaving us alone for ever." Indeed, I believe that the Hound of Heaven, in Francis Thompson's imagery, persists in pursuing us, and never really leaves us alone.

The woman in Rose Macaulay's novel speaks of "the pattern and the hard core" that she "can never make my own: they are too far outside my range. The pattern should perhaps be easier, the core less hard."

Yet Christ translates the pattern and is the guide through a complex range to the hard core. What would be the point of life if the pattern were easier or the core less hard?

Christian, for me, means an acceptance of three elements here: the pattern is not easy, the core is hard, and the grace of God in Christ enables the pilgrim's way in faith, in hope, in love.

The sheer passion of Christian must be recovered if the faith is to seriously activate personal life and be a central force in the life of society. The Christian faith teaches that the cross *is* empty. The Resurrection of Jesus Christ enables us to live in hope instead of existing in despair. Yet Christianity is failing to communicate the reality of the Resurrection.

Linked to this failure is an absence of sheer joy, abandon, and passion. A Christian must be prepared to spill his or her blood for the sake of Christ in a bleeding world. Yet Christians' own blood has become more important to them than the blood of Christ—which means not only the shed blood of the crucified but that of Christ alive in the world, especially the persecuted, the suffering, and the poor. Christians today give so many "little things"—a relatively small amount of money, a little bit of time, an ounce of energy, a shudder of passion, a measuring spoon's worth of love. But one looks in vain for the essential gift, that of self and of life's blood.

How can Christian passion be recovered? Not by global conferences, erudite or fiery speeches, public relations efforts, new leaders at the summit, massive fund-raising, a new curriculum for mass education, or reorganization of the structures of church life.

The "solution" may be found only in showing forth the glory of the Lord in the very living of a Christian life. Showing forth the glory of the Lord means a number of related things. To practice prayer as action, action as prayer. To be really prepared to break one's bones and spill one's blood for Christ—and so, for the other. To comprehend that such a faith is not at all playing church but is indeed a radical, overwhelming, life-changing commitment to Christ that leaves no single part of one's life unchanged. To share in Christ's Resurrection is to find that life—one's own, and the life of society that one indwells—is absolutely transformed.

Christian communication, of whatever kind, has to say this clearly to people. It hasn't. Its work is cut out for it. This is a bread-and-butter issue that is second to none in Christian significance.

IV

Christian: Does It Relate to Life Today— and Tomorrow?

What is "Christian" sexual behavior? Is sex "a black tarantula"?

"Sex is a black tarantula and sex without religion is like an egg without salt," according to filmmaker Luis Buñuel. "In the *Summa Theologica*, Saint Thomas says that fornication between man and woman, even if they be married, is nevertheless a venial sin. Now, I think that's a very sexy idea. Sin multiplies the possibilities of desire." So sexual pleasure is linked with the idea of sin and only exists in a religious context. The sexual act "is an exciting, dark, sinful, diabolic experience," Mr. Buñuel told interviewer Carlos Fuentes in the *New York Times Magazine*.

I wish that everyone could have as much fun with sex as Mr. Buñuel has here. But when I first read Mr. Bunuel's remarks, my initial reaction was that he had probably been listening to too many bishops. Church leaders who view sex as sin have long seemed to be more prevalent, in fact, *than* venial sins.

The equation of sin with sex has been the most banal nonsense, torturing and scarring endless human lives. This horror was done blasphemously, more often than not in the name of God.

Much so-called evangelism has exploited human fears, preached God's hate instead of love, espoused denial and repression in the place of fulfillment, and even heretically implied that one can earn salvation by the act of abstinence, rooted in legalism, instead of by faith. Yet our creation in the image of God includes sex as well as other aspects of our lives. Can sex be viewed Christianly as an essentially healthy and good part of life?

This is a question that is directly related to the present and future meaning of Christian. The theology of liberation, which many people who have not studied it define mistakenly as simply a political statement or one that concerns only the Third World, speaks directly to the question of *interior* liberation for all people.

Personal aspects of living are increasingly seen not as excessively privatized but as parts of the full human dimension. Alienation and exploitation, as well as the very struggle for liberation from them, have ramifications on the personal and psychological planes which, says Gustavo Gutierrez, it would be dangerous to overlook in the process of constructing a new society and a new human person.

Modern man's aspirations include an interior liberation in an individual and intimate dimension as well as liberation from external pressures which stand in the way of his fulfillment. This means more than a social revolution; it means continuous creation in order to achieve an ever more total and complete fulfillment of the individual in solidarity with all mankind.

The goal is the creation of *a new person.* "It is not a matter of 'struggling for others,' which suggests paternalism and reformist objectives, but rather of becoming aware of oneself as not completely fulfilled and as living in an alienated society." The denial of one's sexual rights, indeed sexual identity, stands in the way of "complete fulfillment" and surely bars an experience of "solidarity with all of mankind."*

Narrow legal definitions of sex are fences about the natural play of love, relegating the instinct of mutual pleasure and release to dirt, sin, and guilt.

Haven't we, in any case, called the wrong things dirty? We have permitted war to come into family living rooms, bedrooms, and kitchens in living color, and we looked at it while we ate our meals. Yet most Americans did not ever angrily assert that they were thereby being bombarded by *obscenity*. Nor have we as a nation identified racism or poverty as obscene. This is a society that does tragic things, obscene things; yet it is only the physical relations between human beings—the sexual relations—that we seem to term obscene.

Homosexuals have been viewed as queers—ugly, offensive, mistakes of God's creation—to be laughed at, but never with. Gay was not beautiful. Indeed, I recall how a Los Angeles clergyman informed two male gay people that they were not welcome to worship God in that particular church. Their presence as human beings at the altar, he said, offended other churchgoers.

A woman pregnant outside of marriage was long subjected to society's (and the church's) worst calumnies, dour readings from Leviticus, loss of social respectability, and personality damage resembling murder. A woman in need of an abortion sought out a butcher in private, paid dearly, risked life and limb, and suffered in silence.

A segment of religious tradition negates the ecstasy of love-making; sex is to create babies, it teaches, and people engaged in this activity are not to abandon themselves to lust.

* From *A Theology of Liberation* by Gustavo Gutierrez. Maryknoll, N.Y.: Orbis Books, 1973, p. 146.

The law has mirrored the shadows of such thinking. So we find that, according to state law after state law in America, consensual oral-genital contact—even between married people within the confines of their own homes—has long been labeled "the abominable and detestable crime against nature." Imprisonment for this "crime" has been suffered. The definition of "sodomy" includes fellatio and cunnilingus, forms of love-making preceding, and incorporating, intercourse for countless men and women.

Why do I make a point of emphasizing sex in this discussion? Have I a desire to "shock" people? Am I taking sex out of "context" and giving it too much attention for "Christian" consideration? The point is, *it* isn't shocking; *we* are, if we can be seriously shocked by it. But perhaps some of us are shocked even by life itself.

Christian has sadly become irrelevant, something of a joke, in the lives of many people who have reacted against its frequent double-standard moral taboos and insufferably bad theology. The church can't speak to people unless it comprehends, accepts, and loves them as well as the wholeness of human life. It is the church that made the fatal mistake of defining Christian (in practice) as an hour a week inside a building—an hour unconnected to the rest of common, ordinary life. Such life necessarily includes making a living and—yes, brace yourself—sex.

One has observed the sexuality of many male clergy and their wives with compassion often bordering on pity—a special pity not related to unmarried clergy because the former must epitomize "the Christian family." They were long called to be "examples" of Christian living. This frequently meant suppression of their feelings and a seeming cruel judgment upon those of others.

I remember the perhaps apocryphal story told about the son of a prominent cleric who had gotten a young woman pregnant and then married her under familial constraint.

The cleric's wedding present to his son and hapless daughter-in-law was a pair of twin beds so narrow that two bodies could scarcely fit into one of them.

But a new breath of liberation, engendered largely by the civil rights movement in the 1960s, swept through the air. Wasn't it mere paternalism to assist others in obtaining freedom if one ignored one's own need of it? Women's Lib blew the doors open. Now more clergy wives acted out their long-imprisoned feelings, as did women in denominations that barred them from the full ministry of the church.

What did *self*-identity mean? What did full personhood in the body of Christ mean? What was the real relation of sex to the other parts of human life, of one's own sex to the barriers placed around sexual liberation?

Trying to answer these questions, many Christians, male and female, found that the liberalism or radicalism they espoused in such public matters as racism, war, and poverty did not penetrate barriers surrounding their private lives. Private tended to mean sexual.

It was not license that they sought, but responsible freedom. They cared less for the celebration of self-indulgence than wholeness. Caught up in the public exorcism of social demons, they yearned to banish private ones that stood as symbols of hypocrisy and a double standard in their own lives and various exercises of ministry, lay or clerical. Their theology, which had long been confined to biblical exegesis, public sermon, counseling, and an exposition of the relation between God's Word and human actions in the world, now became steadfastly related to the question of how to live their own lives. The question reached Protestant, Catholic, and Jew.

They saw how sex was grossly misused in acts of violence and dehumanization, and they judged such acts as sinful. But sex itself ceased to shock them. They became aware that human bodies are remarkably identical—the body of a man or of a woman. Only a certain (and limited) number and variety of acts of love-making and sexuality had been devised by women and men throughout history or in the present. Genital hunger was a fact of life. Order was necessary in the matter of feeding this hunger, but one did not want a junta mentality to place authoritarian bonds on sexuality (including sexual fantasy) in order to control and regulate it as well as other parts, individual and social, of human life.

People came to realize that knowing and relating to self —themselves—was organically a part of knowing and relating to other people. The person with whom one engaged in social problems was irreducibly a human being. In order to confront that being's needs and reality in an open and nonjudgmental way, one had also to confront the needs and reality of oneself. One significant aspect of the human behavior of both oneself and other people is inevitably sexual.

Organized religion must surely participate in creating a healthier, more open and honest sexual environment. The situation makes me wish that heavy-handed, frowning, censorship-obsessed men and women would relax their witch-hunts long enough to enjoy a belly laugh about sex. For it is surely funny as well as serious, light as well as ponderous.

A number of controversial films have brought sex out into the open as something *people* do. They indicate that many diverse actions are part of human sexuality, not mere aberations. This suggests that cinematic biography may need to explore sexuality far more candidly and scrupulously than it has in the past in order to reveal authentic character and personality.

The church can no longer play Queen Victoria, sitting back and muttering about morality through thick black weeds. If a church leader is going to speak publicly about the state of morality in the arts or the media, he or she had better have seen the play or film under discussion. In the past numerous leaders have notoriously preached sermons of hellfire denunciation against books that were unread by them as well as against plays and films that they had not, alas, viewed.

The same human needs, desires, and passions that have spurred society's rethinking of sexuality now presage an incipient change in spirituality. Sexuality and spirituality have a good deal more in common than many people like to admit. Indeed, the popular conception of "spiritual being" needs to be enlarged to include people's sexuality.

The recent social ferment in American society dealt with people redefining their own sexuality in radical-personal terms, on the basis of their own needs rather than by prescribed and traditional expectations. This means people really being able more openly to reveal themselves. Such openness takes away the threat of an old stigma, for sex does not have to be seen as such a private thing.

The church has too often remained an institution that tried to break people against its rules. So its very unresponsiveness to human needs has created a widespread condition of *spiritual* repression in many lives. Such disparate phenomena as sensitivity training, the charismatic movement, and the Jesus movement have indicated that numerous people were trying in new and often unorthodox ways to meet these spiritual needs, which could not be separated from the needs and realities of their minds and bodies.

The revival of corporate worship, the single most urgent need within contemporary American Christianity, must involve the senses and the body as well as the intellect. This implies ceasing to choreograph worship so very rigidly that it resists or numbs the spirit. Organized religion's penchant for placing a worshiper's body on a wooden bench for one hour a week is simply not sufficient a worship experience to satisfy a strong spiritual drive.

Although corporate worship must be experienced within some kind of form, it should nevertheless allow freedom of the spirit and the body. This revival has to find people where they are—this includes their sexual identity—instead of only on the basis of what plastic stereotypes they are *supposed* to have in a false lexicon of "acceptable behavior." Communion means sharing with other people as with God—truly honest sharing of reality about oneself and what one yearns for.

The ordination of eleven women to the Episcopal priesthood in the summer of 1974 set in motion new ideas and disturbing feelings. And it raised anew the question: What *is* priesthood?

Dictionaries define a priest as one who performs a sacrificial, mediatorial, interpretative, or ministerial function. Priests are people on whom specific powers and rights have been conferred for the exercise of the ministry; they are divinely authorized to offer the eucharistic sacrifice. The gospel speaks both to personal needs and social justice, and a priest must so communicate its meaning.

New definitions and interpretations abound. For example:

Priesthood as an "area of artistry" is suggested by James Forest of the Fellowship of Reconciliation. "It is an essential art, an ability to show the rest of us that strawberries and us and planet and spider's web and the invention of such words as love and mercy all have to do with—what phrase to use?—the Lord of the flowers, Yahweh, the presence we know as love, as the deep, fear-erasing appetite for justice, the capacity to forgive. It is an extraordinary art to break open the blindness we've inherited. To awaken hope, to give new depth and distance to imagination. To join us to past and possible. To make evident the essence of bread and wine, of water, of syllable, color, hunger, feast. A priest is a guide into essence."

My feeling is that a priest must be less and less a privileged member of an elite corps, more and more a brother-sister in an open community. Priesthood itself cannot be a cause of separation between people, but rather unity. So priesthood must be continuously validated in life, discovered anew in relationship with other people.

By any definition, however, implicit in priesthood—for two thousand years—has been its maleness. The ordination of eleven women to the priesthood is unprecedented—and threatening. Why threatening? Because we fear (1) acknowledging and dealing with the female side of who we are, (2) facing up to and revering the female aspects of God, and (3) the loss of our own massive male power. Yet each of these fears is really a challenge, a challenge that must be met for the enrichment of the priesthood.

"We need women priests, able to relate intimately instead of as remote 'counseling experts,' " one clergyman told me. "Women priests who will be able to touch people and tell them, 'You're important and I care about you.' "

But such a priesthood forces men to examine themselves in an altogether new way. Men who are afraid of the liturgical kiss of peace in the Eucharist, for example, find themselves confronted by the question: "What is struggling inside me to be discovered?"

One of these men honestly explained his fear: "If I should show feeling and emotion in public, and in church, if I should touch or embrace another man or woman, what would happen to my self-respect? The image I like to project? What people think of me? I'm just not free to do it. I'm not free to be myself, to find out who I fully am as a person."

A young United States Navy ensign, taking the stereotypes for granted, assumes that women are always expressing emotion in public and that men would never do so: "If we had women in the navy, could we maintain discipline when a woman cried as an officer told her off? The same thing is true in church. If a woman priest broke down and cried in front of a bishop who was reprimanding her, it would be unfair to all the male priests and would put the bishop in an impossible position. It just wouldn't work."

If we have real fears of discovering a female side within ourselves, seeing a female side to God is even more threatening.

Of course, the Jews were right from the very beginning when they refused to make graven images of God or give God a name. This prevented the development of anthropomorphism that depicted God as male. In Christian art, including Michelangelo and Hollywood biblical films, the maleness of God has been strongly asserted. We've not seen a depiction of God that suggested Lillian Hellman or Helen Keller, Eleanor Roosevelt or Marian Anderson.

God is revealed in the Bible as progressively manifesting power, righteousness, and mercy. Yet the church has made it impossible for a serious view to be taken that God has female as well as male aspects. By demeaning women, the church boxed itself in; seeing anything female in the deity would then have degraded or lessened God.

"We need to get detached from traditional attitudes toward God and sex so that we can think about God's femaleness without the feeling of terror that it's somehow obscene," said the Reverend Priscilla A. Chaplin, the third woman ordained to the ministry of the United Presbyterian Church.

Now we're seeing a female side of God and Christ that we have repressed for two thousand years, finding evidence of it in various references in the Gospels.

Jesus said: "O Jerusalem, Jerusalem, killing the prophets and stoning those who are sent to you! How often would I have gathered your children together as a hen gathers her brood under her wings, and you would not!" (Matt. 23:37)

Jesus wept for Lazarus; he related easily to women as women; on the cross he was neither an angry man nor a stoic. He expressed a feeling of warmth and relationship toward a crucified thief, arranged for his mother's care and tenderly cherished a close friendship, and asked forgiveness of those who tortured and killed him. His male and female aspects were manifested simultaneously both on the cross and in his ministry; he called upon people to repent, zealously overturned the tables of money changers in the temple, yet revealed the capacity to give and receive love.

"Through women priests and those men who aren't uptight about shedding their masculine roles, we'll discover the female side of God," said the Reverend Nathaniel Pierce, a young Episcopal priest. "This will be a beautiful truth. Maybe the rediscovery of the female part of human and divine nature is the new force in the land."

Now we have a fresh opportunity to rediscover God in a wholeness and fullness that we sinfully and arrogantly denied ourselves for so long a time. We need to have our consciousness of God opened up to reality and be liberated from an absurd male chauvinism that wasn't content to stop with men—it had to reach out to include God.

One result of that was the macho rejection of Jesus *as real.* He was considered too compassionate, too feeling, to be a real model for men. This led, in turn, to the widely accepted view that the church itself was for old ladies and children. Men merely ran it, paid for it, and made use of it at will as an institutional vehicle of Establishment power.

A highly interesting corollary of this has been the church's official attitudes toward such questions as war and amnesty. The church tended to support the former and express leery questions about the latter. The male view held that men who refused to fight in a war somehow denied their masculinity; they should be punished. The female view stressed the spirit of love as transcending harsh strictures and passé images of acceptable behavior.

The same depths of feeling can be found concerning the question of poverty and aiding the poor. The male view affirmed that the poor should not be mollycoddled but help themselves, while the female view held out for mercy, healing, and compassion.

Because the priesthood, a masculine holy of holies and the most impregnable of male preserves in history, will open up vast new areas of human anxiety and psychological pitfalls for men when it becomes sexually integrated, the first woman bishop, or the first woman cardinal, will drive some men up the hierarchy walls. But by narrowly limiting the priesthood to men and seeing God anthropomorphically solely in maleness, the church both denied God and came close to committing institutional suicide.

"How profoundly offensive, how humiliating it is to ask whether a woman can have ordination to the priesthood," a Roman Catholic priest told me. "A woman ministerial associate of mine is an ordained Protestant cleric. I respect her intelligence, her warmth, her character—well, her abilities to do the job."

It is well-nigh universally acknowledged that the efficacy of a sacrament is not affected by the character of a priest-celebrant. Yet a number of women in the priesthood have at least suggested that the efficacy of a sacrament may somehow be affected by the priest's gender.

The idea of receiving the Host from the hand of a woman apparently confronts them with grave difficulties. The matter of kneeling down before a woman to receive the sacramental Body of Christ is laced with ambiguities for a number of male critics, whose opposition up to this point has been admittedly jejune.

Could this stem from the life experience of praying "Now

I lay me down to sleep" and later "Our Father who art in heaven" while one was mentally on one's knees before a male God? Certainly the male priest before whom one knelt in church to receive Holy Communion was a surrogate figure of that same bearded and patriarchal God.

Women, too, are victims of this indoctrination. One, after seeing the ordination of eleven women to the priesthood on TV, said: "Women priests are disgusting. One of them cried. Priests shouldn't cry. I wouldn't let one of them inside my front door if she came to call."

Yet Christian baptism means complete, not partial, church membership. Any kind of churchly caste system is on the shakiest theological ground. A baptized Christian—female, male, white, black, gay, Chicano, Japanese, Native American—is equal to any other baptized Christian as a member of the Body of Christ. Period. Digression from this truth is heresy, and so help us God, the church itself carries on heresy, in the very name of God. Even children—children of both sexes—are victimized by sexual segregation of acolytes at the altar, for these are almost inevitably boys.

The church cannot speak effectively to society, and especially its youth, as long as it maintains a caste system and denies the meaning of both baptism and civil rights to anyone. That's what drives millions of people away, while an outmoded and unloving institution spends millions of dollars on "evangelism" designed to bring people into its tired ranks. The institutional church often seems like a medieval pope, clothed in furs and hanging with jewels, trying to make up the princely mind whether or not to turn the next dismaying corner into the preceding century.

A measure of the church's grave difficulty at present is found in this comment from a lawyer and businessman who is a lifelong Episcopalian: "I have no feeling as to whether priests should be men or women. It's the same thing for me; we no longer need priests of *any* kind. It's better for people to help themselves, to do what needs to be done in their own communities. I don't trust or respect priests, female or male. Why should I? I certainly don't need a priest to get me to God."

A woman minister said that "We don't need big daddy anymore to pull us out of scrapes." We need to grow up, she explained, and added that "maybe earth mother isn't too good either."

The meaning of baptism, coupled with the realities of civil rights, will inevitably settle the question of women's ordination on the side of women. Changing minds and hearts will take a while—it might not happen until people experience God through a human being whose female side is dominant.

But to storm the walls of the priesthood is a revolution in the relations between the sexes. For when a priest is a woman, even God is no longer a male. Then we must *really* see that our rigid sex roles are to be discarded, for we are persons with acceptably different parts of our natures—and we are free even as God is free.

What does it mean to be a Christian today? This is a bread-and-butter issue for me. I see fragmentation at many levels of the contemporary Christian experience. For example, there are sharply contrasting definitions of prayer, worship, the experience of the Holy Spirit, social action, the proper relation of church and state, Christian sexual behavior, sacred and profane, violence and non-violence.

Take prayer. One view of it holds prayer in a pattern of supplication, awe, propriety, ineffable mystery, and a formless mystical chasm between God and a pray-er. Yet for others, authentic prayer is personal, without a trace of separation from God. It can express deep outrage, virtual disbelief in the God who is being addressed, an absence of all acceptable propriety including the pose of loving, and can be uttered in generally socially disreputable language, even including what are oftentimes called obscene words.

In her book *Widow*, Lynn Caine describes her feelings as

her husband died slowly of incurable cancer. From the depth of her agony she railed at God, swearing in her utter frustration and lashing out with passion. Then she cried:

> "Let him stop fighting! Let him die! Let me get on with life! I was daring God and I knew it. I didn't know how I could live after Martin died. All I knew was that I had to. I had two small children—Okay, you smartass God up there, what *will* become of me? You don't have any answers, do You? And You're supposed to be so almighty!

Lynn Caine is engaged in prayer—sweaty, earthy, naked, unorthodox. It is not at all unfamiliar to God, even as it surely offends the ears of numberless faithful churchgoers.

Let's take a look at Christmas as another example of the fragmentation of contemporary Christian experience. I asked a number of people to tell me what Christmas means to them.

R.W.B. Lewis of Yale, author of *The American Adam*, put it this way: "Christmas, for me, is partly nostalgic— memories of going through the snow to midnight mass in the church of which my father was pastor. The present reality is mainly familial—the month-long period culminating in Christmas week when the family draws closer together, parents and children hold whispered conversations and think lovingly about one another. But there is something more. I'm not much interested any longer in the theological aspects of Christmas. Yet the occasion is much more than a holiday. I feel something ritualistic and celebrational in the air, an obscure sense of promise renewed."

But a black teen-ager in a poverty area of Los Angeles said, "What does Christmas mean to me? Nothing."

A woman in Boston threw my question right back. "Christmas is nothing but commercial now. I don't know what it means. *Tell me.*"

A workingman in Houston told what Christmas means to him: "A rest. Ten or eleven days off at the factory."

A sense of an actual spiritual vacuum at Christmas was explained by a teacher in Chicago. "I become depressively lonely," he said. "My soul has a deep need to feel a depth of joy, but I can't find it. The last time I went to church on Christmas I walked out in a shaking rage. We drive Christmas away from us by making our observance of it such a big lie."

Most people with whom I talked concerning Christmas were sharply critical of its present practice as grossly commercial. They felt this deprived it of profounder meanings.

A rabbi strongly called for reaffirmation of these meanings. "Without hope, humanity dies," said Rabbi Balfour Brickner, director of the Department of Inter-religious Affairs, Union of American Hebrew Congregations. "Where are the words, the ideals that will make us more human, less brutish? As a Jew, I draw inspiration from my own Jewish tradition. Chanukah, a festival we celebrate also at this time of year, draws me again to the realization that the condition of freedom, so essential to creative life, must be fought for vigorously and guarded with utmost zeal. Christmas, for one tiny moment in time, brings its adherents to focus on the rebirth of hope in a world where such traditional values as trust, belief in one another and in one's own capacity to do and be better, desperately awaits the brightening polish of Christmas."

Another prophetic voice breaking through superficial practice to essential Christmas meaning was that of Martin E. Marty, the theologian, church historian, University of Chicago professor, and associate editor of *The Christian Century*: "The inventors of Christmas were disturbers of the peace. Before tinsel and cherubs distracted, they shocked the world with the message that God dwells with people in Jesus Christ. Men and women, despite them-

145

selves, began to see need around them, darkness in their own souls, and hope from unexpected sources—all because God had positioned himself so strangely at the center of the human drama.

"My Christmas will not let me chatter about the Prince of Peace until I discern what the war has been about; it will not let me hear that 'Christ is the answer' until the questions first shatter me. And if creative disturbance comes, *then* let me join those who sense the first fresh hints of shalom."

At least two youths related Christmas to simple joys within the family circle. A college freshman in Alabama held this picture of the season: "It's a nice time. People come together. In the family circle you can see distant relatives again. It's not necessary to get presents for everybody to be happy."

A tenth-grader in Georgia looked forward to seeing Frosty the Snowman on TV. "I want to see if he's the same as when I was smaller. And I want to look at pictures on TV of little kids getting toys at Christmas, and a lot of lights and snow. Decorating people's homes is fun, too. At Christmas I enjoy myself."

Yet another teen-ager in the inner city of Detroit held different memories. "When I was very, very young, Christmas meant getting up in the morning and wanting gifts that wouldn't be there."

Sister Jean Marie Bartonek, a Roman Catholic nun in Los Angeles, offered this poignant view of the meaning of Christmas for her. "I like to run to Bethlehem, curl up in the corner of that stable and be safe. As a modern religious I have recently emerged from a highly structured, protective environment into one much less secure. I am like an infant attempting its first hesitant steps. But the thought of Christmas banishes my fears and gives me direction. Christmas is a time of heart. It is touching base. It is a reconciliation with hope, and the recovery of faith and courage. To me, it is *love* renewed."

A teen-ager in Washington, D.C., offered a personal view of Christmas that was a compelling testament of significant human relationships. "Christmas is a kind of dream," he said. "When everybody gets together for Christmas, if only one person who should be present isn't there, then it's not really Christmas."

There used to be a collective center, and people paid lip service to universal symbols and accepted truths. Now these are subjected to hard scrutiny by people acting individually as well as belonging to identity-bestowing classifications of race, sex, ethnicity, and life style. When people change, so do their images of Christmas as visible signs of questioning or belief. What Christmas means to people significantly reflects the deep changes in their experience and practice of life.

I have tried to define what Christmas means to me in two prayers that I wrote concerning Christmas. The first prayer focuses on Jesus:

It's Christmas again, Jesus.

So we're going to celebrate your birthday another time around. But are we aware you're *real*, Jesus?

I mean, do we honestly accept your humanness as well as your being the Lord? I don't think so. Maybe this is why we seem to be despising humanness pretty generally in our world right now.

Thank you, Jesus, for your life as a baby, a growing boy, and a man. Thank you for respecting and loving our humanness so much that you have completely shared it with us.

And thank you for being real, Jesus. Please help us to understand what it means to be truly human and real, with you and the others we share life with.

"Silent Night." The nights I know, Lord, are noisy and frantic. Be there with me in the noise and confusion, will you, Jesus? Happy birthday—I hope it's okay to say that to you, Lord. Thanks, Jesus, for being our brother as well as our Lord.*

The second prayer that I wrote about Christmas focuses more on ourselves, how we might practice Christmas more creatively and honestly:

It is Christmas again, Lord.

Save us from being selfish at Christmas. Help us to give freely and joyfully of ourselves to others who are in need.

Vivify our thoughts as we recollect your birth, Jesus. May the poverty of the manger be etched deeply on our consciousness. We live today in a world still marked by poverty, hunger and dreadful need. Grant us compassion and love, Jesus, and appreciation that you share life with us.

Beneath the din of blatant commercials and cash registers, help us to know what Christmas really is.

Thank you, Lord.

As I see it, we've come to take for granted a season full of simple and complex meanings that we have lived with all our lives. So the jubilation has gotten lost in tinsel; mystery has been tarnished by malpractice; and love edged aside by the almighty dollar in the wondrous act of giving. It's no surprise that there is a sense of heightened sadness and loneliness for many people at a season that has all too often lost its way, denying its source of love and true sharing.

To me, Christmas means to let the sunshine in—awaken to the unbridled joy of salvation and the splendid freshness of eternal meaning.

Other people's reminiscences about Christmas remind

* From *Malcolm Boyd's Book of Days.* New York: Random House, 1968, p. 211.

148

me of my own youth. When I was in high school, several of us—girls and boys—used to go shoplifting together. We hoped that it might relieve our boredom and the sense of despair that we felt even then about growing up in a world whose manifold problems dampened our zest for life.

What elaborate plans we made. First we would visit shops that seemed likely prospects for our adventure. On the appointed day one of us would engage a clerk in conversation. The others, wearing loose-fitting raincoats, would quickly pick up items that were desired. A pewter tray. A bottle of cologne. A sweater.

Our exit would be a masterpiece of timing and deception. Back in our car, laughing almost until we cried, we would divide our loot. We didn't need it, you understand. All of us had money to buy whatever, within reason, that we liked. But we defined our action as adventure and fun, as we did a weekend night's game of strip poker.

Morality was an abstract word in a dictionary for us. We believed that it didn't relate to *real* life. In *real* life war was glamour ("Alexander's Ragtime Band . . . come on along, come on along"), poverty was the fault of poor people, black people were niggers, a career was a means to an end ("but work, work hard, real hard") and the end-all was personal security and affluence. It was assumed this purchased freedom.

Religion was paying lip service to an impersonal and remote God. One went to church, heard a lot about Jesus but could never understand him, prayed for things one wanted, and then hoped for ultimate mercy instead of a burning hell at the end; but that was a long way off.

What does religion mean in today's America and world? When I was asked to consider the idea of writing a weekly column about religion for a newspaper syndicate—an idea that was later discarded—I turned to a friend for his qualified advice. He is an influential and highly respected U.S. newspaper editor. *What* should I write about if I accepted the column assignment, I asked.

His thoughtful reply, based on informed insights about the making and working of society, told me a good deal of what religion means today in the eyes of the American public.

These were his suggestions:

1. Religion as an elite, ingroup activity. Over the past twenty years worship has gone from being something nearly everyone does to something that hardly anyone does. Highly differentiated sects of militant activists, fundamentalists, pentecostals, all-round conservatives, liturgy freaks, and whatnot seem to be emerging from what was once the amorphous glob of the American Protestant-Catholic-Jewish scene.

2. The communes that survive. I've read more than I want to about communes and how tough it is to make a commune go. Nevertheless, the Hutterites and the Doukhobors and the Bruderhoffs have survived for decades. Some parallels here should be of interest.

3. I didn't raise my kid to be a hippie, says the old man of the now-aging hippies. Now we've moved along to the point where hips are parents, too. How are they raising their kids? Are these offspring of the counter-culture any different from my own three children eighteen to twenty years ago?

4. One of the toughest jobs must be that of the war chaplain. How do you talk love and salvation to a guy who has just shot up a miserable village in a war that is condemned by a large chunk of the world, including his own church, his family, himself?

5. The irony of celibacy. The conservative Roman Catholic hierarchy is obsessed with fending off assaults

on priestly celibacy while at the same time, celibacy, as much as any other factor, seems to enable the Berrigans and their like to act without regard for personal security. They don't have to worry about family, mortgages, school bills, etc.

6. Hallelujah, brother!—James Cone at Union Theological suggests that blacks may have a monopoly on the Christian message of our time. More than just that old-time religion; aren't the blacks the real Christ figures of our day?

7. Whatever happened to pornography?—it's not dead yet, certainly, and pornography will always be with us, but the fast-buck stuff is losing its appeal. Hardcore films with flimsy plots that a few months ago brought $5 ticket prices in New York, $4 in nearby cities, now are being advertised at 99 cents. Magazine racks are loaded with dozens of one-shot efforts that aren't moving. We're satiated. Too much of a bad thing?

8. Getting more out of giving. (A United Fund luncheon prompts this.) United Funds, churches, charity campaigns in general, are finding a growing resistance in these days of the tight dollar. How can giving become more meaningful, more rewarding, less a sandbagging, resentful operation?

9. The new missionaries, those going out of the Interchurch Center in New York with mandates to be disc jockeys, literary experts, film advisers, God knows what. (More your stripe, Malcolm, and less Norman Vincent Peale.)

I appreciated the editor's suggestions. They helped me immeasurably.

But I asked myself yet another question, one having roots deep in the American religious situation. What of youth? I believe that one must seriously try to understand the drives and feelings, the nature of experience, and the goals of young people of the new age in which we live. Christian impulses run deep in the age's too readily apparent contradictions between violence and love, compassion and overwhelming anger. I learned a good deal about this during an event that transpired in New England over a few spring days at the start of the 1970s.

"Don't read the news—make it," announced a scrawled sign atop a padlocked newsstand near Yale University, during the "May Day," 1970 weekend rally for support of the Black Panthers that drew fifteen thousand outside visitors, along with national guardsmen, to New Haven amid rumors of violence and the rhetoric of revolution. I was in residence at Yale as an associate fellow of Calhoun College.

Four thousand Army paratroopers and marines were flown to New England to stand by in the event of violence, when Attorney General John Mitchell granted a request made by Governor John N. Dempsey of Connecticut.

"Z" was painted on walls around the Yale campus. Many students, drawing an analogy between the plot of the prizewinning Greek film and events in New Haven, feared that a nonviolent student political protest would be met by an Establishment-provoked incident leading to serious repression. Such fears were exacerbated by the announcement of U.S. military intervention in Cambodia.

Would an attempt be made, during the eclectic weekend assembly, to "tear Yale down," as colorful posters suggested? No one knew.

The first day of the assembly was peaceful. Thousands of students sprawled on the New Haven Green, across from the Yale campus, listening to rock music and speeches. A copy of of Malraux's *Man's Fate* lay beside a sleeping student. Many turned on by smoking pot. ("Arresting us for smoking dope is like arresting Jews for eating matzoh," Jerry Rubin, the Yippie leader, told a group of Yale students. "Five hundred thousand young people have been locked up for smoking the flower. Alcoholics have been arresting pot smokers.") One male youth stripped naked and danced, reminiscent of Woodstock.

Early that evening, I walked onto the Old Campus, an area where freshmen were housed. A rock band was playing. Lights shot through the darkness, playing over a thousand students seated on the grass.

"We've failed," a Yale student disconsolately told me. "We're damned if we do and damned if we don't. If we have a bloodbath, the Panthers are hurt, the blacks suffer as usual, and Yale is discredited. But if we have a rock festival and smoke pot—like we're doing—we don't win anything. It's hopeless."

Rock played loudly in the background as I asked another Yale student what were the reasons for the student strike, the assembly and the outpouring of feeling.

"It's not the reasons we've announced—freeing Bobby Seale who's on trial, or building a day-care center for blacks, or giving money to the Black Panthers for a defense fund. It's despair. We've been programmed all our goddam lives. The computer has got stuck. We're so goddam frustrated we can't stand it. Then last night Nixon said we were going into Cambodia. Man. We don't want what America seems to want. And we're so goddam boxed in."

A Yale student and his wife told me they were going to Canada because of his draft status. "But we're not afraid," his young wife said. "We're ready to start a new life there."

There was a pause, and then her husband softly told me, "It's rage we feel. And we don't want it to destroy us. You don't fight rage with rage. You try to get well."

A few moments later, the peaceful night had changed into a nightmare of sound and fury. Hundreds of students joined arms and marched down Elm Street toward the Green. Many shouted "Sieg Heil!"

"Goddam fascists," said a Yale professor as he stood by, watching them.

What had happened, like a rapid brush fire, to alter the situation? Someone had announced to a crowd of students that four black youths had been arrested on the Green. The reaction was sudden and violent.

Yet the announcement, we learned, had been false. The Black Panthers, alarmed by the lie that could result in considerable damage to their cause, worked for an hour to turn back the crowd. Neither guardsmen nor police appeared, and peace seemed finally to be restored.

But a small group of youths—perhaps fifty of them, white visitors to New Haven from outside—marched down College Street to confront the police. They hurled rocks and bottles at the guardsmen who, after repeated barrages, responded with tear gas. Two blocks away, our eyes stung as the gas reached us in the courtyard of Calhoun College. Again and again, the youths charged and the guardsmen used more gas.

Finally the night's tumult ceased. But the next morning, tear gas still lingered in the streets and on the grass in the Green, causing irritation to one's eyes and throat.

In mid-afternoon, back on the Green, there were speeches again. The rally on the Green ended peacefully. I was seated with a group of fellows and students in the Master's House of nearby Calhoun College when clouds of tear gas swept through the college gate from Elm Street. We ran to close windows. Within a few minutes the empty courtyard seemed to be filled by dense mist. More than a hundred students required medical assistance, with a few needing psychiatric counseling.

Now tear gas seeped through the closed windows. We felt the irritation of it and worried as the peculiar odor of gas grew constantly stronger. Instead of relief, more and more tear gas was fired directly outside the college by guardsmen at a group of gas-masked, out-of-town young visitors ("provocateurs," the Black Panthers called them) who would not give up the fight.

Yale's chaplain, William Sloane Coffin, Jr., described

them later as "a small group of irresponsible, irrational, and violent outsiders, all of them white, who were made that way, in large part, by the irresponsible, irrational, and violent policies of the United States."

Now we heard yet another bulletlike sound, indicating that even more tear gas had been fired into the crowd. So the gas continued to swirl around us, turning the night air gray and sinister. Hours later, peace had come to the streets.

Both the rhetoric, and the compulsion to violence, of a hard core of whites shattered a tentative view of American revolution—along lines of *Battle of Algiers* images—previously held by a number of Yale students.

"I don't believe in the kind of violence I saw in the street last night," a self-styled radical white Yale student told me early Sunday morning over a cup of coffee. "I've got to rethink what radical means. I think maybe I'm a liberal and damned proud of it. But I don't want just to work within the present political process and participate in demonstrations. It has to mean more than that. I wonder if liberals don't need to quit feeling guilty and start taking the offensive. To be a liberal and not run away but just stay there, and tell both right and left to make plenty of room for you—that may be the thing to do."

Although the students didn't know it at the time, their world had just changed significantly. So had they. Millions more students similarly changed after the public events of the late 1960s and early 1970s that painfully included the shooting of students at Kent State University in Ohio. For one thing, they would not again be so vulnerable, so innocent. In the future they would take a more practiced, if cynical, view of establishments and revolutionaries. They would inhabit the former more than the latter; their habitation of establishments would be revolutionary in character rather than stance, for already they were agents of fundamental change.

As they moved further and further away from recogniz-

able religious imagery or words, so they would earnestly—
even passionately—seek unnameable Christiań virtues in
their lives: honesty, fidelity, meaning, and hope.

Their own movement away from any form of organized
religion—which would continue to move away from
them—was matched by the growing fragmentation taking
place within religion itself.

It seems to me that at least five separate blocks emerged
in American religious life in the early 1970s. First, established religion that was defined by denominational organi-
zations. Second, anti-Establishment religion, ranging from
individual theologians to charismatics, from the gay church
to Jesus youth. This bloc was under a big umbrella; its com-
ponent parts did not relate very much to one another.
Third, a group of social activists who found the roots of
their social conscience in the Judeo-Christian tradition but
later withdrew from an interest in, or the practice of, religion. Fourth, cultists who manifested genuine spiritual
hunger while being disinterested in the churches. They
identified with oriental gurus, meditation exercises, astrol-
ogy, magic, the occult, communes, special diets, and/or
other aspects of contemporary spirituality. Fifth, the indif-
ferent. Their biblical and theological illiteracy grew as fast
as their own numbers. I found that separation between
people in these blocs was hardening. The resulting fragmentation resulted in more and more people talking only to
themselves in small ghettos while denied communication
with others having different religious, spiritual, or moral
experiences.

For example, a significant segment of Roman Catholic
priests who married, in opposition to their church's regula-
tions, simply dropped out of the life-style marked by church
attendance. A number of homosexuals living in major
urban centers established a new pattern of separatist
churchgoing.

The Episcopal church's institutional refusal to admit

women to the full ministry of the church threatened anew the meaning of catholicity, increasing the possibility of further fragmentation in the form of a moral reaction against such an institutional decision.

A number of social activists, generally young men and women, left churches that opposed granting amnesty to young men who became resisters or deserters in opposition to the Indochina war, and changed the public focal point of their idealism from a religious organization to small, grass-roots sociopolitical bodies centered on specific community goals. And all the time—owing primarily to past and present segregationist housing and school policies—blacks and whites continued a widespread pattern of separatism to worship.

What, if anything, could be done to alleviate the present situation? In the past, shifts in forms of religious organization—including proliferating denominations—took place as human responses were made to new situations and needs.

Today thousands of Christians accept a denominational label out of old habit or for sometimes obscure purposes of identification. They pay lip service to a form of religious organization but lack a worship experience that is vital and strikes an answering chord at the center of their lives.

Too many of today's Christians are like the abbot in *The Catholics*. The abbot played an assigned role, but he did not pray, did not commune deeply with God. He acted out his public role stoically, by rote based upon obedience to institutional authority. However, spiritual juices no longer ran in his body, mind, and soul. A double standard, a conflict between one's outward profession of religion and inner practice of faith, renders a person dishonest. And this state can produce feelings of unbearable frustration and guilt.

Is there a possible alternative—one that could free latent, repressed spiritual energies and make room for an honest religious creativity of the kind that is now denied a large number of Christians?

There are varied prophetic impulses in contemporary American religious life. At their best, these witness to the breaking of new ground in the life of faith. Each has its shortcomings, yet each meets needs of people whose spirit has been bottled up and denied institutional manifestation. Many who stand in the mainstream of "middle religion" are cut off from such examples of overt experiment and radical risk. That is why these prophetic impulses need to be embraced by the catholic church, not suffocated or welcomed paternalistically.

Might a new and alternative organization of Christians become a sign of the church's catholicity by bringing together people who are now separated but need one another as brethren in Christ? Mutual isolation cuts off spiritual interaction for worshipers, segregating them into ever more sophisticated ghettos. Can ethnicity and conviction alike be shared in love?

If so, then it would be no longer necessary for many women and men to tell and live a lie, within the structured body of Christ, concerning their own nature and identity. Love, with its powerful capacity for healing, would no longer be denied to particular people on the basis of their skin color, their gender or sexuality, their ethnicity and politics, even their resistance, as individuals created in the *imago dei*, to the arrogance and tyranny of human institutional conformity.

Every class needs to meet another class inside the church; the young need to meet the old; threatening images need to come together in the emerging form of fellow human beings. This is especially important at a moment in history when the reality of community is lacking; for genuine community can witness to spiritual and moral roots and possibilities.

Demagogues traditionally flourish in a condition of communal rootlessness and breakdown. If a common Christian experience of history, doctrine, piety, and tradition is not witnessed to, one can only anticipate—with dread—the rapid development of self-interested parodies of serious theology and the utter negation of prayer.

In 1944, Ignazio Silone remarked poignantly that "In the sacred history of man on earth, it is still, alas, Good Friday." In the same vein, A. Alvarez, in his book *The Savage God*, spoke of a numbness "beyond hope, despair, terror and, certainly, beyond heroics" as "the final quantum to which all the modish forms of twentieth-century alienation are reduced." He identified "an art which forces its audience to recognize and accept imaginatively . . . the facts of death and violence." Yet our destiny is not to linger in fire-lit darkness, for the end of our journey is the center of light.

God addresses the separated segments of the church in numerous ways, taking on the guise of "other" voices, "other" needs, and "other" persons. Where established denominations remain insulated from new religious stirrings and impulses; where new movements tend to be self-righteous, ingrown, and lacking in a sense of historical and spiritual continuity—there perhaps a solution must be sought in a new and alternative organization of Christians. The present American crisis calls for moral and spiritual fire. The Spirit of God ignites that fire within the consciences of women and men who may be required to redefine the meaning of Christian community in this age.

One such man, a prophet and a priest for modern America, was Martin Luther King, Jr. He also became one of modern America's victims.

The mystery of Martin Luther King's life and work continues to deepen with the passage of time. Either he is enshrined as a kind of plastic black-and-contemporary Christ figure in an irrelevantly distant hall of fame, his image warmed by an eternal flame, or else he is deemed to be a tragic man who fell out of step with his times, failed to construct a viable political organization, and even misunderstood the nature of realistic black aspirations.

Like John F. Kennedy, King is now more myth than

man. If he had lived, King would have celebrated his forty-sixth birthday in 1975. It is apparently easier for people to place King in history—as a folk hero, devil, or saint—than to live with what he literally represents and still has to say. Those who understand this, and oppose the thrust of King's beliefs, seek to keep his tomb closed. They are right in realizing that a resurrection could be dangerous to them. King is as unyielding in death as he was in life when it comes to resisting the self-conscious seduction of radical chic and the easy popularity of accommodation to predictable demands.

The zeitgeist, the spirit of the time, buoyed King at the beginning of his mission. It called for racial integration, openness between blacks and whites, and nonviolent demonstration by civil rights activists to arouse world moral opinion against traditional power structures that relentlessly supported the sociopolitical-racial status quo.

As King later recalled in his book *Stride Toward Freedom*, it was on a cool Saturday afternoon in January, 1954, that he set out to drive from Atlanta to Montgomery and his destiny. Soon he would be grabbed and molded by the pull of events outside his basically religious and scholarly life. The crisis of the Montgomery bus boycott, and the role that he was given in it, would transform him into an international personality.

Ironically, at a time when many people would shortly declaim that they did not trust or want leaders anymore, Martin Luther King became a leader. He appears to have been a faithful one. He did not lose touch with his constituency of common people even when it sometimes lost patience with him.

King was one of the last epic leaders. Critics who believed that he was dictatorial in his organizational methods labeled him "De Lawd." Others felt that his charisma, employed for the sake of touching the consciences of masses of people, was neither a weapon nor a gimmick, and they wished to follow him.

160

What was King's message? On one occasion he put it succinctly in these words: "Men often hate each other because they fear each other; they fear each other because they do not know each other; they do not know each other because they cannot communicate; they cannot communicate because they are separated."

However, in the mid-sixties the zeitgeist, the spirit of the time, shifted. The earlier mood had generated a spiritual adventure in search of honor and even a moral certainty of victory. But hopeful expectations had been dealt deadly blows in the highest seats of government, in the nation's cities and suburbs, in the North and South.

Soon the cry "Black Power!" replaced the song "We Shall Overcome." Integration came under attack from many blacks and those whites who were in the vanguard of fashion. It was said that in the integration movement whites controlled the traffic and selected the vehicles, with these whites half-stepping in double time. Antiwhite feeling was met by a stronger white backlash that resisted black demands for social change.

However, King now moved against separation. The clean line of simplicity in his message was not simplistic. He dealt with the universal and undying themes of survival, justice, and love. A reading of his last book, *Where Do We Go From Here: Chaos or Community?* reveals that he understood intimately the dynamics of both black and white power, the grievances that logically provided the rationale for black separatism, and the full dimensions of white racism.

This must have been a painful and lonely period for him, especially when he further isolated himself from the mainstream of opinion by denouncing the relation between poverty ghettos in America and battlegrounds in Indochina. "The *Washington Post* has calculated that we spend $332,000 for each enemy we kill," King announced. "It challenges the imagination to contemplate what lives we

161

could transform if we were to cease killing." His attack upon the Vietnam war brought him rebukes from prominent blacks as well as whites.

The way King was lionized after his death clouds the reality of the harsh rejection that he suffered earlier. For example, I remember an incident in Mississippi in the summer of 1965. One afternoon I was with a group of young black SNCC workers. King's face appeared on a TV set. "Turn it off," shouted someone angrily. The others felt the same way; the set was abruptly turned off.

Many whites, at the same time, were calling King a "Communist." It was several years after King's death that Lt. Gov. Lester Maddox of Georgia raised ghosts of the past when he expressed opposition to placing King's portrait in the Georgia Capitol picture gallery.

"I don't think we have any more business putting Martin Luther King's picture up there than Gus Hall's," said Maddox. (Hall was chairman of the American Communist Party.) Maddox charged that King's "efforts did more to spread the cause of communism and socialism than any Georgian ever to live."

Standing firm against calumny and fierce opposition, King remained committed to both racial integration and nonviolence. He said that he would rather be a man of conviction than conformity.

King saw integration as "genuine intergroup and interpersonal living." He found that "there is no separate black path to power and fulfillment that does not intersect white paths, and there is no separate white path to power and fulfillment, short of social disaster, that does not share that power with black aspirations for freedom and human dignity."

He spoke poignantly, and almost in a Pauline spirit, of nonviolence as "a conviction so precious and meaningful" that he would "stand on it till the end." Violence, he wrote, was "a descending spiral, begetting the very thing it seeks to destroy." He believed that hate cannot drive out hate; only love can do this. Racism he defined as "total estrangement." With nonviolent resistance, King noted, "no individual or group need submit to any wrong, nor anyone resort to violence in order to right a wrong."

Martin Luther King never offered anybody a rose garden when he spoke of racial understanding. It is something, he said, that we do not find but must create. The answer to the racial dilemma, he cautioned, can be discovered only "in persistent trying, perpetual experimentation, persevering togetherness."

These remain the truest words I have ever heard on the subject. They are based on the belief that blacks and whites, given all the exigencies of history and the differences that exist between Euro-Americans and Afro-Americans, do share a common destiny.

I was in the same room, or on the same road, with King many times. Generally he was in front, marching or speaking; I followed or listened to him. His energy seldom deserted him in such public situations, yet I never had the impression that he was turned on in a show biz sense. He seemed to be all of one piece, possessing the rarest of qualities which is integrity, along with limitless patience under the tug and pull of constant pressures.

In September, 1961, King sent members of his staff to instruct twenty-seven of us—blacks and whites—in the philosophy and techniques of nonviolence before we commenced a "prayer pilgrimage" freedom ride. After that I was with him on several occasions in the deep South taking part in various demonstrations. Then I recall chatting with King on the day before he was named recipient of the Nobel Peace Prize.

Somehow I remember most vividly a spring day in 1965 when a large number of blacks and whites jammed Brown's Chapel in Selma, Alabama. I was among the "outside agitators" who had responded to King's Macedonian call to come

163

and help. Looking tired but confident and assured, King was on the platform. I watched him closely from where I sat in a front row.

He exhorted us to action.

"It's better to go through life with a scarred body than a scarred soul," he said.

How can I explain, without sounding absurdly maudlin and sentimental—and if I do, what the hell—how his words brought quick, hot, embarrassing tears flowing from my eyes? King touched a supposedly hidden nerve in that area known as my conscience. He conjured up at least a glimpse of vestigial innocence deep within me. So ideals were possibilities, and pragmatic ones. He roused my weary body and soul to renewed action. He stirred impulses that warred against my narrow self-interest and fear of an involvement that could be costly.

"We must meet violence with nonviolence," he said. Here was the hard core of the controversy that at least temporarily earned King the censure of that season's young, black militants as well as many unsure, imitative white liberals—yes, including myself—who worked with them.

However, at this moment the intense crowd inside Brown's Chapel in Selma was carried along on the emotional wave of King's conviction and strength. He seemed to be consumed by a fire that burned deep within his soul. There was something of a young Moses about King as he taught and led us, struggling to make us want to reach the promised land that he saw. But he knew how long and hard that passage would be. Many followers would fall away, losing their stamina and ceasing to share his dream.

"Pilate's great sin wasn't that he didn't know what was right but that he lacked the moral courage to stand up for right," King thundered from his pulpit. He knew the ambivalence of the world's Pilates, past and present, in the face of life's myriad wars and Watergates, betrayals of the poor, and price tags placed on justice.

"I would rather die on the highways of Alabama than make a butchery of my conscience," King as a prophet said. When he later died in Memphis, I believe that his conscience was intact.

But he was down when he died. Down in popularity polls, acceptance by U.S. presidents, and cheap esteem. Everybody seemed to see King differently and make their own demands on his conflicting imagery. People tended either to feel furious or else simply let down whenever King refused, or was unable, to perform according to their stipulations. The immense irony of the drama *Rashomon* was writ small in his own life.

King will stand, in my opinion, as a more lasting figure in American history than any U.S. president who served in his lifetime. For he addressed directly and creatively the American dilemma, its racial sins, and its possible cure.

Long-range results of his work can already be seen in present American life. Derivation of it, for example, was the coalition support and election of Maynard Jackson, Jr., and Coleman Young as the first black mayors of Atlanta and Detroit, respectively.

Indeed, Mayor Young said in his inaugural speech that Detroit "has too long been polarized. . . . We can no longer afford the luxury of hatred and racial division. . . . What is good for the black people of this city is good for the white people of this city."

I saw another outgrowth of King's work in the memorable and statesmanlike remarks offered by Rep. Andrew Young when he explained why, with decidedly mixed feelings, he cast his vote in favor of Gerald Ford as the vice-president of the United States.

I know now how little I really understood Martin Luther King while he lived among us. I want to know him a lot better, stay behind his ideas and help to make them work, and also let his own actions continue to inspire my life.

The struggle for freedom and justice continues. Civil

rights is not dead, but alive. White liberals must cease agonizing about their popularity ratings with a broad cross section of blacks, and get on with the job that is unfinished. It is a job that King shared with blacks and whites alike, and he asked for the support of both.

The last time I was with King was in a nonviolent protest against the Vietnam war. On February 6, 1968, King joined several hundred others of us in Washington, D.C., to demonstrate for peace. We stood together inside Arlington Cemetery, directly below the Tomb of the Unknown Soldier. A federal appellate court had rejected an appeal for permission to hold a formal memorial service for the war dead. Therefore, we stood silently as we prayed for peace. At the head of our group two men could be seen, one carrying a Torah and the other a crucifix.

I took notice that King's spirit had not flagged. He was still Brother Martin, the leader, as he infused us with renewed enthusiasm and vigor for our common task. Then, as we departed, one of those inexplicable coincidences that make perfect sense occurred. A carillon in the cemetery chimed the hymn which is a paean to unity and against the evils of separatism, "In Christ There Is No East or West." It was a poetic good-bye to Martin Luther King. I had, of course, no way of knowing that the occasion would mark my good-bye to him as well.

King embraced East and West, being enabled to perceive Gandhi as a contemporary saint. His words and actions cut to the heart of the meaning of Christianity. King exposed alike the hypocrisy of a self-serving practice of religion that affirms only personal salvation while it looks away from social ills, and the arid sectarianism of a social gospel torn from its spiritual and historic roots. What he stood for may well represent the last chance for Christianity to be a way of life, a living religion, in the twentieth-century world.

Why is it that so many so-called Christian leaders, unlike

King, do not seem to understand Jesus at all? They seek to lock Jesus Christ inside stained glass and dogmatic formulations. But he gets away, eluding their keys and chains. King held onto the central message of love even when virtually everybody wanted to ridicule him for doing it; and he turned away from easy secular acceptance, embracing unpopular doctrines and causes while his esteem declined. Essentially he had a true sense of Christ; he really seems to have understood Jesus Christ.

Adolf Holl writes in his *Jesus in Bad Company* that Jesus developed an unusual sociogram:

> Those addressed are asked to give first preference precisely to those groups they have thought of least, and if at all then only as enemies. Thus the forgotten and the enemy are pushed into the normative position: we are asked to consider them and to see them as base in our consideration of others. Social behavior is to be determined not by elites or majorities but rather by the poor, the mournful, the hungry.
>
> But Jesus' "attempt to bring about an aggression-reducing change of direction through a movement downwards has not come off; the medicine he prescribed has never been taken."

The major churches long ago rechristened the real, disobedient Jesus (Holl observes), making the official "church" Jesus generally popular among representatives of power. Yet the real Jesus "wants to change thought, not direct it along new lines that would simply become another rut."

King, I believe, saw through the sham of the official "church" Jesus and accepted the yoke of the real, faithfully disobedient Jesus. When Billy Graham has long been consigned a footnote in the social history of America at mid-twentieth century, King will be remembered by Christians

167

wherever they inhabit the earth as a disciple of Jesus Christ who stood in the way of the cross.

A bread-and-butter issue for me is: How does Christian relate to life tomorrow?

What determinative form may Christian faith take in the future? Two novels, the first published in 1959 and the other in 1974, speak more prophetically about this subject, in my opinion, than anybody else does.

Both novels move against a background of apocalyptic events that have shattered structures of society and plunged human lives into disastrous straits. Walter M. Miller, Jr.'s, *A Canticle for Leibowitz* depicts a monastic community far in the future of time; it tried to preserve both devotion and learning within a disciplined common life but is embattled by furious forces that would destroy it and imperil the whole of human life as similar forces have already come close to doing centuries before.

Thomas S. Klise's novel *The Last Western* also portrays the future, although the settings as well as the forms of social tumult are familiar in a rather contemporary mood. Foreign wars rage, sapping lives and energy; domestic cities are in permanent civil conflict, with authorities battling guerrilla insurrectionists; bread and circuses are offered to the populace as mighty sports events in great stadiums; institutions continue to be self-interested—the church, for example, is almost entirely identified with the Establishment and against poor people. But in the midst of this situation, Klise introduces us to a monastic community, the Silent Servants of the Used, Abused, and Utterly Screwed Up.

The members of the community do not speak but use sign language:

> The reason for using sign language was set forth in the Guidebook which had been left by the founders of

the Society: *Men have created a false world with words, which they use to cover up their sin. Better the language of deeds, of loving and serving those who have been crushed by the words of the world.*

All words are lies, someone had added in red ink.

And someone else had added an entry in purple crayon: *Even these words.* *

But sometimes the community held listening services. A passage of Scripture or a portion of the guidebook was read. Or, a brother or a sister would tell a story, perhaps one of personal conversion, in sign tongue. Then all would listen in silence, contemplating its meaning, "letting it enter." Then the Servants would share the fruits, or *dona*, of their contemplation, more often in sign than words. This, in order to share "pictures, dreams, visions."

The guidebook contained this "recommendation" as one of its earliest entries:

> The Servants will always choose the way of serving the poor, the lonely, the despised, the outcast, the miserable and the misfit. The mission of the Servants is to prove to the unloved that they are not abandoned, not finally left alone. Hence, the natural home of the Servants is strife, misfortune, crisis, the falling apart of things. The Society cherishes failure for it is in failure, in trouble, in the general breaking up of classes, stations, usual conditions, normal routines that human hearts are open to the light of God's mercy.†

I find the mark of Christian upon this community of Servants in Klise's book. The mark of Christian is the relation-

---

*From *The Last Western* by Thomas S. Klise. Niles, Ill.: Argus Publishing Company, 1974, p. 132 and p. 150.

† Ibid.

ship between a person or a community with Jesus Christ. He lived and died without secular power. He called society to judgment and redemption. He evidenced a clearly alternative life-style. He was executed by the state. Indeed, Jesus simply doesn't fit at all neatly into the modern Establishment church as we know it. Even now, however, one recognizes the presence of Jesus Christ in scattered pockets of humanity, in experiments of love and justice, in efforts to achieve communities, and in various human groupings that bypass the citadels of self-contradictory power in the world.

I am intrigued by what Arnold Toynbee, writing in The *London Observer*, had to say in the spring of 1974 concerning the circumstances surrounding a possible resurgence of monastic life:

> A society that is declining materially may be ascending spiritually. Perhaps we may be going to return perforce to the way of life of the first Christian monks in Upper Egypt and of their sixth-century Irish successors. The loss of our affluence will be extremely uncomfortable and it will certainly be difficult to manage. But in some respects, it may be a blessing in disguise, if we can rise to this grave occasion.

In the Third World most Christians—at least those standing outside of institutionally powerful roles—have no affluence to lose. This is a part of the fragmentation of Christian experience in today's world, where Christian may hold vastly different meanings for a disciple in, say, Latin America, Africa, or the United States.

The ironies of living in such a complex religious era, where even what is patently labeled as nonreligious is filled with religious yearnings, were urgently revealed to me when I dined one night at the Drawbridge restaurant in Northville, Michigan. It is a former church.

The restaurant was "transformed into a latter-day castle

by adding an honest-to-goodness moat and drawbridge to a 19th-century landmark church," according to *Signature*, May, 1974. "The church interior was preserved, complete with carved ceiling, aged stained-glass windows, pulpit and balconies, and medieval touches—arms and armor, heraldic decor—did the rest."

Dining inside the old church I noted the place of the former altar, which was still marked. The gourmet dishes included risotto frou-frou (tenderloin tips with pineapple, banana, and curry sauce; I ordered it and it was very good) and red snapper fingers with artichokes. Glancing up, one caught sight of the old choir loft, which now houses a bar. Stained-glass frames the scene; a sense of post-Christianity is in the air. But maybe Jesus was here in a sense that he was not in a "real" church up the street.

"He's seldom seen in churches, for there he's worshipped anyway," Adolf Holl states. "He dresses unobtrusively and never wears a uniform. And he never stops anywhere for long."

Our concept of religious imagery may be in a healthy stage of evolutionary development. Seemingly we seek to inhibit Christ less claustrophobically. We have come to recognize piety in the marketplace and on the street, not merely inside a church; and we have been enabled to discern the face of Christ in other human faces, especially those of the suffering, the persecuted, and the poor.

Recently when I visited an art museum I saw a cross. It was a processional cross, of tempera and gold on wood, made by Neri Bicci in the fifteenth century. It stood upright in a guarded glass case inside the museum. The familiar figure of Jesus crucified was on the cross, with his arms stretched out and his hands nailed down.

Did I find Christ on the cross? No. He seemed to be outside of the glass case and in the lives of a museum guard, a couple looking at a man nearby who had been created by Giacometti, a young woman seated on the gallery floor gazing at a drawing of an aged man and woman, and me. Also, here as at the Drawbridge restaurant, Jesus seemed to be quite freely engaged in the lives of people.

Millions of earnest women and men struggle in the tortured wasteland of American religion. Caught between the Scylla of the institutional church and the Charybdis of Grahamistic "American religion," these people resolutely seek new alternative structures and forms in which to celebrate their faith. They behold the spiritual odyssey as panoramic, embracing the vast totality of organic life and death, Pope John's soul, Martin Buber's soul, Martin Luther King's soul, a universal dream, and the risen Christ.

Epilogue

I look back on years that seem innocent in their hope for the future and evil in their masking of awful realities.

How am I to be labeled? As white, male, American, *and* Christian. I also am a New Yorker in exile. Raised on the island of Manhattan from birth until the age of twelve, I listened to Uncle Don and Chandu the Magician on the radio, read "Little Orphan Annie" and "Dick Tracy" in the funny papers, ate Wheaties as a youthful disciple of Jack Armstrong the all-American Boy, lived inside an urban cave called an apartment. I visited the aquarium and there acquired a sea horse, "Hippocampus Hudsonius," my "Rosebud"—which still patiently stays with me, preserved under glass in a small case. From time to time I return to the city, exteriorly a visitor.

Manhattan, its skyline punctuated by towers as its truth by fables, has stood friendly or brooding beneath sunshine or mist to receive me, a recurring prodigal, into the furious flow of its existence. On one of my cyclical returns to the city, after an absence, I saw the then new Empire State Building for the first time. I looked up self-consciously to behold this giant. It confirmed a heady feel of the city's—and one's own—power, a curious sensation of security.

However, the sky creature born of technology also communicated to me a queer sense of unease. Was it a latter-day Tower of Babel (which I had learned about in Sunday school), and might God lash out in a fit of wrath (as in certain descriptive passages of the Bible, also learned in Sunday school), raining death and destruction over the city's streets as retribution for supreme arrogance?

In life-style I am a highly mobile person. Interiorly, I am not a stranger to restlessness either. I have been forcibly struck by Karl Barth's "There is suffering and sinking, a being lost and a being rent asunder, in the peace of God."

A lovely incident, during a trip to Israel, served memorably to underscore this fact of my life. One afternoon I visited a distinguished Jewish theologian in his Jerusalem home. He received me graciously as a guest—an American Christian who had written a book of prayers entitled *Are You Running With Me, Jesus?* We enjoyed an hour of conversation. Suddenly, I glanced at the clock and realized that I was late for another appointment.

"I must run," I exclaimed.

"God has placed a curse on you for writing that book," he said levelly, with only the slightest suggestion of a smile at the corners of his eyes. "God will make you run forever." He put his arm around my shoulder, and we both laughed. I shall not forget our meeting, particularly when I am harassed, under pressure, and running.

As an uprooted New York child, I spent some time in Texas and Oklahoma. Once I attended a revivalist's meeting held in an enormous tent in Tulsa. When the revivalist called for converts, I walked forward, my heart in my throat, straight up a sawdust-covered aisle. Later I returned home and explained that I had been saved, only to be informed by irritated adults that I was *already* saved, baptized in a church, and would go to my prosaic Episcopalian Sunday school as usual on the next Sunday as if the untoward incident had not happened.

Another Sunday morning, when I played hookey from that same Episcopal Sunday school (for the day was already hot and sticky), something occurred that I shall never forget. With a couple of friends of mine, I wandered up the street to a house that was directly alongside a Baptist church.

This morning the lady of the house—call her Mildred—was suffering from a pleurisy attack. Her husband sent one of us boys for the doctor. Meanwhile, however, Mildred had decided that she was actually dying and, to judge by what we heard through the open windows, was going through a classic deathbed scene.

When the doctor came at last he perceived immediately what was the matter. He prescribed a tablespoon of gin every two hours for relief of the pain. Mildred was a teetotaler, but her husband told her that in this case the gin was medicine, and, wishing to arrest her pain as quickly as possible, he gave her a whole cupful of gin instead of a mere tablespoonful.

A couple of hours after Mildred's husband had commenced this treatment, people began arriving for worship at the church next door. Presently the opening of the service was clearly audible through the church's wide-open windows. By this time Mildred felt no pain. In fact, she was in a state of utter euphoria, and apparently she felt a need to share her joy with everybody else. At any rate, when she heard the minister start preaching his sermon, Mildred raised her voice in "Bringing in the Sheaves." She belted out the song contrapuntally to the minister's exegesis.

Later, when Mildred had fully recovered from her pleurisy attack, no one ever mentioned the incident to her. She continued to abhor the use of alcoholic beverages. So far as she knew, no strong drink had ever passed her lips to mar her chances of salvation. As for me, a young witness of Mildred's deathbed and salvation drama, I found religion altogether remarkable and certainly not in the least dull.

I have never been able to settle for a too easy definition of religion. In my experience religion is mystifyingly divisive as well as unifying, harsh and gentle, alternately warlike and peaceful (with the former emphasized at the election of a bishop). While it points toward life after death, it is concerned with the intricate warp and woof of *this* life—with war, with racism, with sexual habits and human alliances. Far from proffering elysian fantasies, religion often seems hell-bent on a collision course with serenity.

I remember one crazy confrontation with at least the trappings of power. It was in Washington, D.C., in late 1969. The war in Vietnam stretched on, and the bombing continued unabated in its fury. Several of us decided to enter the Pentagon and, once inside, to conduct a Peace Mass in a crowded corridor of that warrior's holy of holies.

We were approximately forty people—men, women and children, clergy and laity—belonging to a peace fellowship. Our group had begun to gather outside the Pentagon when I realized that, God forbid, I had to urinate. Awareness of a forthcoming long bus ride to jail intensified that need, which was shared by a student in our group. He and I decided to stroll casually through the Pentagon doorway and look for the closest men's room. Upon entering the Pentagon, however, we walked up one corridor and down another, around this corner and the next, but in vain; we could not find a lavatory.

I was wearing vestments for the Peace Mass—a white alb that reached to the floor, and over it a chasuble with peace symbols embroidered on it in flaming red and yellow. The male student at my side had long hair—a bit longer, it occurred to me, than Vanessa Redgrave's in *Camelot*—which cascaded over his shoulders halfway down his back to the jeans he wore.

"Why is everybody staring at us, Malcolm?" he suddenly asked me.

Just then we found a men's room. As we walked in, we

encountered some fifty men standing before two straight rows of urinals. The sound of water was like a miniature Niagara Falls. When the men saw us, a mass movement ensued; the sound of water stopped, zippers were closed in a quick, cinematic style, footsteps raced to the door, and within what was surely only seconds the student and I stood alone inside that room. Power had reacted to us; a form of communication had taken place.

The student and I rejoined our group. We held our Peace Mass. It was interrupted by the police, who arrested us for "disturbing the peace" and carted us off to jail. Our poignantly harmless liturgy occurred on a day when U.S. bombs fell by the thousands on already war-scarred Vietnamese victims. Next day and for days after the bombing of Vietnam continued; we had not been able to stop it.

However, while confronting that strange complex known as the Pentagon, I learned anew that human beings, with personal tastes and feelings, honeycomb even the most bureaucratic of institutions. On that occasion a government attorney, assigned to the case against us, asked to see me inside the jail to which our group had been taken.

The setting he chose was another men's room. He apologized for belonging, as he put it, "on the other side." Yet he wanted me to know that the book of prayers I had written was a source of continuing "spiritual use and inspiration," as he described it, for both his wife and himself. He said they kept the book on their bedside table.

So I learned once again that "the enemy" is not categorically the enemy, any more than "allies" can be counted unambiguously as comrades. There is too much mystery and paradox in life for simplistic truisms. When one has stripped power of its mystique, its robes and artifices, it becomes vulnerable as a network of pompous-humble, unyiedling-communicative, and inevitably human people. When you stand up to power, you stand up to one or more individuals. Look an individual, then, in the eye. Laugh, if you feel like it; this may rightly be received as a much-needed expression of human solidarity.

Another learning experience came to me when I addressed several hundred white Protestant high school students at a church meeting several years ago. I attempted to establish creative rapport with these students, in the hope that this would set up dialogue between us. But they were unyielding and frozen—largely, I think because a number of their adult teachers were also seated inside the auditorium, scattered among the youths.

Failing to break the ice at all, I finally said, in jest as well as frustration: "All right, tell me about your sex lives." No one breathed. One could have heard a pin drop.

"Do you ever pray?" I asked.

"Yes," voices cried out. "Constantly." "All the time." "Several times a day."

"To whom do your pray?" I inquired.

"God!"

"Who is God?" I asked.

"He's the biggest there is." "The strongest." "He is the wisest." "He is white."

One of those students very seriously told me: "You can't call Jesus Christ your personal Lord and Savior unless you hate communists and would kill one."

I wondered about organized religion and what it has done, in various places and times, to people in the name of God. *Can* religion be "contained" within a rigid, powerful, self-perpetuating institution?

This question was rather cruelly brought home to me in 1965. I worked that summer in the civil rights movement in rural Alabama. My companions were four young black men. We slept at night on country shack floors. We ate once a day when a poor black family shared its meager rations with us. We experienced the ironies of law and order—for example, when we drove in Mississippi ten miles below the speed limit so as to avoid any confrontation with local police; yet our car containing four blacks and a white was spotted as a civil rights vehicle, and we were arrested for—it was a lie—"exceeding the speed limit."

When that summer's first Sunday morning rolled around, I thought I would go to church. This necessarily meant entering a building and participating in the activities there. In such a building, however, blacks were not permitted to worship God with whites.

I asked myself hard questions: Did God require (want) me to leave my four young brothers, with whom I shared the danger of death, in order to offer worship to him in a racially (humanly) segregated ritual? Indeed, did Christ come to people in that community only in the form of a communion wafer that was consecrated by a duly ordained minister of a traditional rite? Or was God free, and greater than the stipulations even of highly religious men who were institutional racists?

In the end I spent that Sunday morning sitting quietly with my four companions inside a rural shack, drinking coffee and eating toast. And I held the sure conviction that God was with us, and that Christ freely came to us sacramentally in the form of our bread and drink. This awareness shattered forever the rigid doctrinal structures that had previously existed in my consciousness.

I reject the self-righteous claims of both half-moons, the social gospel and the personal gospel. Each is inadequate without the other. You can find, on the one hand, bitter and spiritually dried-out activists who do not pray and, on the other, poseur pietists who do not give a tinker's damn about their neighbor. Christ is reduced by both to a perpetual caricature of an angry young man overturning money changers' tables inside the temple; or else he is locked inside a stained-glass window—where, blue-eyed and blond-haired, he gazes limply at the dew-wet grass at his bare feet.

It is the gospel of Jesus Christ that commands my loyalty,

my imagination, my love. Today we are at a turning point in history, a time when we dare not abandon or betray that gospel. We cannot let connections to tradition and historical spiritual experience be snapped. Nor can we permit "do-it-yourself religion" to change the universal church into mere proliferating house-churches where bathtub theology is manufactured instead of the prohibitionist's bathtub gin, where instant gods are created in the images of men and their ideologies, where the Judeo-Christian social ethic becomes a lost dream, and prayer is speaking to oneself.

I feel an urgency concerning my commitment to Christ. Once, during an afternoon's discussion at Yale, I spoke about the peace movement and expressed sentiments of self-criticism from within that movement; wherefore someone angrily turned on me and said: "Damn it, can't you wait until we win?"

I realized then, as I do now, that the answer is no. I can't wait because I may be dead tomorrow and not have a chance to speak and act. Acting immorally in the name of morality is abhorrent to me. Indeed, I must turn the question round and ask, "What does it mean to win?"

The years have taught me the cost of getting involved in life. It is all a risk. One is on stage in an ever new set without a script. The floor may give way without warning, the walls may abruptly cave in. One may die at the hand of an assassin acting on blind impulse. Security, for which men sell their souls, is one of the few real jests in life. The cost of not getting involved in (anyone else's) life is higher; one has merely died prematurely.

People have been my teachers. They have taught me by their frowns, smiles, silences, appetites, superstitions, beliefs, loves, hates, costumes, masks, gods, lusts, ideals, and hopes. Now I finally know how to accept happiness. In one way or another, happiness invariably involves other people.

In the process of living these fifty years, I have come to know success intimately. (Failure, another close friend of mine, is success in the buff, bare-assed and streaking.) Having been burned badly by success on one occasion or another, I decided henceforth not to play casual games with it. Yet I have a voracious appetite for experiences with success.

But I ask less and less of success now. One cannot serve two masters—success knows that as well as I do. However, when occasionally I still find myself locked in fierce combat with success, and it appears to be winning—trying to convert me to its prestigious and glittering mini-deities—I am greatly assisted in my struggle by recalling that the central success symbol in the world is Jesus' wooden cross.

As I look back over my life (curiously, I am now one-fourth as old as the United States of America) I realize that I was always more like *The Glass Menagerie's* Tom, who was "pursued by something," than like a young knight consciously searching for the Holy Grail.

My own strife is not yet over. My personal battle is not yet won. But I know that Jesus Christ has completed the strife for me. Alleluia. He has won the battle. Hosanna.

Shalom